ELECTION NIGHT NEWS AND VOTER TURNOUT

Election Night News
— and —
Voter Turnout

Solving the Projection Puzzle

William C. Adams

LYNNE
RIENNER
PUBLISHERS

BOULDER
LONDON

Published in the United States of America in 2005 by
Lynne Rienner Publishers, Inc.
1800 30th Street, Boulder, Colorado 80301
www.rienner.com

and in the United Kingdom by
Lynne Rienner Publishers, Inc.
3 Henrietta Street, Covent Garden, London WC2E 8LU

Library of Congress Cataloging-in-Publication Data
Adams, William C.
  Election night news and voter turnout : solving the projection puzzle /
William C. Adams.
     p. cm.
  Includes bibliographical references and index.
  ISBN 1-58826-381-9 (hardcover : alk. paper)
  1. Election forecasting—United States. 2. Television in politics—United
States. 3. Voting—United States. 4. Mass media and public opinion—United
States. I. Title.
JK2007.A33 2005
324.973—dc22

                                                              2005000397

British Cataloguing in Publication Data
A Cataloguing in Publication record for this book
is available from the British Library.

Printed and bound in the United States of America

     The paper used in this publication meets the requirements
 ∞   of the American National Standard for Permanence of
     Paper for Printed Library Materials Z39.48-1992.

 5 4 3 2 1

Contents

List of Tables and Figures   vii
Preface   ix
Acknowledgments   xi

1   The Controversy's Context, 1960–2004   1

2   Reassessing Conflicting Findings   23

3   Election Night Newscasts   39

4   Polling Portland's Nonvoters: Western Oregon   59

5   Turnout Test of Twin Counties: Eastern Oregon   75

6   Heartland Not Disheartened: Idaho, Kansas,
    and North Dakota   85

7   Decades of Dinnertime Dropoff: California   95

8   Deploring but Ignoring Projections: Washington,
    Oregon, and California   103

9   Sorting Through 2000 Snafus: Florida   113

10   Equity, Fairness, and Policy Options   127

References   137
Index   145
About the Book   149

Tables and Figures

Tables

1.1	Projections in Pacific Standard Time, 1960–2004	2
2.1	Effects Summary	25
2.2	Effects Summary for Survey-Based Studies	30
3.1	Election Projections and Exhortations in the 1984 Portland News Media	44
3.2	Leading Portland Radio Stations	47
3.3	1988 Election Projections and Exhortations	49
4.1	Comparative Diffusion Rates	66
4.2	Main Reason Cited for Not Voting	68
5.1	Comparison of Malheur and Grant Counties	77
5.2	Late-Day Hourly Turnout in Oregon's Malheur and Grant Counties	81
6.1	Similarity of Matched Comparison Counties	88
7.1	Los Angeles County 6:00–8:00 P.M. Turnout as a Percentage of All Votes Cast	98
7.2	Los Angeles County 7:00–8:00 P.M. Turnout as a Percentage of All Votes Cast	98
9.1	Florida-Related Chronology	114
10.1	Policy Proposals	131

Figures

1.1	Cumulative Electoral Votes, 1984–1988, by Hour Most Polls Closed in Each State	4
1.2	Cumulative Electoral Votes, 1992–1996 and 2000, by Hour Most Polls Closed in Each State	5

1.3 Times When States Were Treated as "Projectable,"
1960–2000   6

1.4 Times When States Were Projectable with Size
Proportionate to 1984–1988 Electoral College Vote   7

1.5 Cumulative Electoral Votes, 2004–2008, by Hour
Final Polls Close in Each State   8

1.6 Final Poll Closings by State with Size Proportionate
to 2004–2008 Electoral College Vote   9

1.7 Maximum Exposure to Projections When Networks
Wait Until All Polls Close in Each State   10

1.8 Voter Turnout Trends Based on Voting-Age vs.
Voting-Eligible Population   13

1.9 Fifty Factors Suggested as Influencing Voter Turnout   16

1.10 Model of Factors Potentially Influencing Voter Turnout 18

1.11 Isolating Potential Projection Effects   19

2.1 California Population, Voting-Eligible Population,
and Registered Voters, 1970–1982   27

4.1 Cumulative Diffusion of Projection News Among
Voters and Nonvoters   63

4.2 Sources of Projection News   65

5.1 Matched Oregon Counties   76

5.2 Cumulative Hourly Turnout as a Percentage of All
Votes Cast   79

5.3 Late-Day Hourly Turnout as a Percentage of All
Votes Cast   80

6.1 Matched Idaho and Kansas Counties   87

7.1 Los Angeles County Turnout in Major Projected
Elections   96

7.2 Los Angeles County Turnout in Projected vs.
Unprojected Elections   97

7.3 Los Angeles County Turnout in Off-Year, Projected,
and Unprojected Elections   100

9.1 Los Angeles County Turnout in Republican Precincts
vs. Countywide   116

9.2 Margin of Victory by Time Elapsed Before
Median Projection Broadcast by State   121

Preface

Since the 1960s, Americans have debated how much damage is done when TV networks proclaim the next president while polls in the western states are still open. The controversy was reignited in 2000 by unjustified projections and again in 2004 by exit polls leaked prior to projections. Past academic studies, rather than settling the debate, have produced conflicting findings. This dispute is particularly interesting:

- as a practical political problem—because, if critics are correct, projections could decrease voter turnout and reverse the outcome of close legislative races
- as an interdisciplinary question—spanning sociology, mass communications, political science, journalism, psychology, public administration, applied statistics, and public policy
- as a multifaceted methodology challenge—coping with less than ideal measurements while trying to detect what may be a small but important impact
- as an unusual public policy matter—bringing research to bear on the merits of competing legislative proposals
- as a purely normative issue—involving questions of fairness and equity in a democracy

Taking a close look at the controversy, the goal of this book is to develop a more comprehensive understanding, if not resolution, of the central issue: do projections decrease voter turnout?

Acknowledgments

First things first, and that means thanking and recognizing those who made this book possible. All those thanked below deserve the usual exemption from any shortcomings in the text, which are my full responsibility.

Outstanding survey coordinators in Oregon included Kristine Alward, Lee Braymen-Cleary, Bill Lingle of Linfield College, David Cassidy of Pacific University, Merlin Douglass of Portland Community College, Tom Kruse and Pam Wilson of the Oregon Health Sciences University, and Kirk Flanders of Lewis and Clark College. The Oregon research was also facilitated by the help of Michael Cox, Vicki Ervin, Carol Voigt, Robert Markham, Bob Crane, and Les AuCoin and his staff. For the election night use of telephones, thanks are due to Linfield College, Phillip Knight, and Nike Inc. Survey coordinators in Washington, D.C., were Tim Klein, Leslie Suelter, Tonya Smith, and William Vantine. Dan Perrin provided helpful Florida documents.

The late Ted Smith III, an exceptional scholar and friend, offered greatly appreciated advice. Warren Mitofsky originally suggested the valuable idea of a large election night survey targeting nonvoters somewhere in the West (the basis for Chapter 4). Working with Leanne Anderson, Jason Cook, and Shena Redmond of Lynne Rienner Publishers has also been helpful.

At George Washington University (GWU), special thanks go to Director of the School of Public Policy and Public Administration Kathy Newcomer, along with other outstanding past and present GWU colleagues including Mike Harmon, Lori Brainard, Jennifer Brinkerhoff, Bayard Catron, Donna Infeld, Steve Chitwood, Dwight Cropp, Phil Joyce, Jill Kasle, Jed Kee, Roz Kleeman, Cynthia McSwain, Phil Wirtz, and Mike Worth.

An important debt of gratitude is owed to GWU research assistants Karen Bland, Liz Barron, Matt Crouch, Nate Crow, Mark Duffy, Tara

Hill, Bob Jones, Tim Klein, John Mahoney, Michelle Mrdeza, Mary Beth Morgan, Mercy Viana Schlapp, Sofie Chen Shen, and Bruce Wartell.

Additional thanks and recognition for volunteer telephone interviewing go to volunteers from Lewis and Clark College including Ernst Aebi, Denis Arnold, Kenneth Blum, Beth Davison, Margaret Fine, Jacqueline Gerome, David Hoffman, Paul Johnson, Theodore Jones, David Marrier, Linda Pitcher, Laurie Underwood, Charles Veigel, and Neil Vollen.

Callers working with the team from Pacific University included Karie Adams, Ralph Browning, Julie Burton, Kathy Coffman, Cathy Crapson, Bob DeMoss, David Dutra, Svetlana Filer, Eileen Fletcher, David Husk, Jill Kaady, Robert Kiepke, Leslie King, Kelly Krautscheid, Penny Lasko, Lee Lewis, Elizabeth Lipke, Frederick Speck, Sharon Trimble, Joni Utterback, William Waldo, Lisa Webber, Gregory Weber, and Douglas Wilbur.

At Linfield College, interviewers included Kevin Baum, Michael Beirne, Andrea Bergstrom, Kim Boye, Suzanne Brice, Timothy Clark, Caitlin Cuddihy, Tracy Davidson, Timothy Dennis, Greg Duncan, Mark Elzie, John Ficken, Nancy Fisher, Steve Holdt, Teresa Howell, Katherine Huit, Kathryn Karr, Julie Marletto, Debra Miller, Melvin Murphy, Julie Olson, Robyn Perry, Lucille Preiss, John Prevedello, Andy Ross, Brad Snodgrass, Amy Spreadborough, Scott Stoddard, and David Tarabochia.

Other volunteers in Oregon, including faculty, staff, and students from Portland Community College, the Oregon Health Sciences University, Reed College, and other interested citizens, were Holly Barker, Robert Belcher, Rachael Berber, Ghaery BonDurant, Donna Borst, Amy Brooks, Elaine Bueffel, Perry Carlson, John Cleary, Melody Cleary, Doris Cleary, Mark Freeman, Marisue Gage, Kevin Grimes, Liane Hirabayashi, Mary Hull, Diane Jelderks, Cheryl Jelderks, Jean Johnson, Connie Johnson, Brian Malley, Elizabeth Marshall, James McCarthy, Evelyn Mundinger, Helen Nahstoll, Mark Nelson, Betty Price, Rachael Price, Heidi Pronath, Pam Ramsey, Pamela Reed, Bernette Ronfeld, Shawn Samuth, Robert Sax, Cynthia Sax, Steve Sheldon, Meri Taylor, Douglas Towne, Colleen Utter, Athena Wang, Dick Young, and Barbara Young.

Working on the same election night survey from telephone banks loaned by Peter Hart in Washington, D.C., were GWU public administration graduate students Thomas Cove, Betty Beuck Derbyshire, Richard Derbyshire, Sharon Duffy, Kenny Gruder, Scott Hieber, Loren

Hocking, Amy Kovler, Deborah Lesser, Lauren Meschler, Wilke Nelson, Shari Spitzer, Nina Weisbroth, and Neil Weiss.

A partial listing of GWU undergraduates who participated in the election night survey includes Betsey Bancroft, Marcela Cintron, Betsy Cohen, Ed Deiss, Jill Edy, Felice Elefant, Bruce Flax, Jennifer Frans, Cindy Glanzrock, Kenneth Gold, Steven Goldner, Brian Gruber, Rudi Gruson, Greg Guastamachio, Anthony Harris, Kathy Hill, Elena Hirshman, Ron Hutzler, Keith Jacobs, Dolores Jalbert, Jerry Jones, Robert Kalok, Jacqueline Kay, Melanie LaForce, Janet Lychork, Michelle McGee, James McKnight, Jim Moninger, Meredith Moss, Cathy Natelli, Carrie Netting, Becky Reeves, Becky Roberts, Caren Rubin, Catherine Spaur, Molly Stauffer, Brad Sussen, Ann Sweeney, Jodi Talentino, Lisa Turner, Warren Warsaw, and Stephen Wyman.

Graduate students in my course in research methods and applied statistics who offered especially helpful comments on draft chapters included Marguerite Bogle, Kate Coventry, Rachel Lynn, Tanya Qadir, Rebecca Singer, and Rebecca Triche. Others who helped indirectly but importantly included Magda Bagnied, Tom Berryman, Lyle Brown, Bob Darcy, Chris Edwards, John Fisher, Eric Fox, Carolyn Hayes, Bob Lichter, Bob Lippard, Kathy Reed, Rosemary Smith, Dennis Sorro, Bonnie Perry, Steve Perry, Frank Turek, Ron Zink, and Sallye Zink.

In an era of interest group–funded research, it is important to note that no research funding was received from any partisan, foundation, or media sources. The sole financial support was a small grant from George Washington University's Committee on Research, at a crucial stage in the project, thanks to the strong support of Susan Tolchin.

This book is dedicated to my three extraordinary nieces: Crystal Reed, Kelly Reed, and Lindsey Reed Dickinson.

—Bill Adams

1

The Controversy's Context, 1960–2004

From Maine to Hawaii, it is election day. Americans are choosing their next president and many other officials. It is 6:00 in the afternoon on the West Coast where voting is under way for another two full hours. Many people are stopping off to vote on their way home from work. Yet by this time, the winner in the race for the presidency already has been proclaimed—in 1996, 1984, 1980, 1972, 1964, and 1960—by at least one major TV network. Potential voters have by now been told, in the words of Dan Rather (CBS in 1988): "It's over."

Such projections have become common. In eight of the twelve presidential contests from 1960 through 2004, the winner was announced before polls closed on the West Coast. Landslides were not required. Only the very tightest races (1968, 1976, 2000, 2004) have not been called early (see Table 1.1). The routinization of projections did not make them any less controversial. Angry officials in the West have continued to insist that projections discourage many people from voting and thus are

- "stealing votes,"[1]
- "threatening democracy,"[2]
- "a slap in the face to Western voters,"[3] and
- "appalling and totally irresponsible."[4]

1

Table 1.1   Projections in Pacific Standard Time, 1960–2004

Year	Race	Mean	ABC	CBS	NBC
	Election day, Tuesday P.M. PST				
1984	Reagan-Mondale	5:14	5:13	5:00	5:30
1964	Johnson-Goldwater[a]	5:24	6:21	6:04	3:48
1972	Nixon-McGovern	5:53	6:20	5:50	5:30
1996	Clinton-Dole-Perot	6:00	6:00	6:00	6:00
1960	Kennedy-Nixon[a]	6:17	7:33	5:14	6:03
1980	Reagan-Carter	6:33	6:52	7:32	5:15
1988	Bush-Dukakis	6:43	6:21	6:17	7:30
1992	Clinton-Bush-Perot	7:48	7:48	7:48	7:48
	Wednesday A.M. PST				
1976	Carter-Ford	12:35	12:30	12:46	12:30
1968	Nixon-Humphrey-Wallace	6:52	5:19	7:45	7:33
2004	Bush-Kerry	Kerry conceded at 8:05 A.M.			
2000	Bush-Gore	No unretracted projection.			

Sources: Postelection issues of *Broadcasting, Time, Washington Post.*

Notes: West Coast polls close at 8 P.M.

a. Projections in 1960 (and to some extent in 1964) were often not stated as firmly as those in later years. The less formal early styles emphasized "probability" with increasing certitude over the course of the evening.

Exit Polls and Time Zones

How have early projections become possible so often? Projections, one critic quipped, are the culmination of journalists' wont to "get drunk on polling."[5] Drunkenness aside, it is true that rapid projections are made possible by exit polls—interviews conducted randomly with thousands of voters at selected precincts across the country during election day. When exit polls show a clear pattern, the networks "call" that state as soon as all or most of its polls close.[6] When a state's tilt is less clear, exit polls are supplemented with actual ballot counts as soon as precinct tallies begin to be released.

Using these data to project individual states, the networks can often rapidly forecast the nationwide winner because so many heavily populated states are located in the eastern and central time zones and close their polls by 8:00 P.M. Nationwide, most states close their polls at 7:00, 7:30, or 8:00, excepting three states that close polls at 6:00 P.M. (Indiana, Kentucky, and Hawaii) and three that keep polls open statewide until 9:00 P.M. (New York, Rhode Island, and Iowa).[7]

Most states close all their polls at the exact same time. At that instant, TV networks treat those states as eligible to be projected. Prior to 2002, in states where polls were not closed uniformly, the networks tried to call such states as soon as most of their polls closed—even if some polls remained open. This approach meant that several states with two time zones—Florida, Kentucky, Michigan, Indiana, Kansas, Texas, and Idaho—were often projected soon after polls closed in the more populated eastern time zone, despite ballots being cast for another hour in the western zone.[8] This was a standard network practice for decades until it was abandoned as one of the reforms following the Florida projection fiascos of 2000.

Together, these four elements—exit polls, states' poll closing times, the "most polls closed" shortcut, and the electoral vote concentration in the eastern and central time zones—made it possible to declare the winner early in the East Coast evening (8:00 EST) when it was 5:00 PST on the West Coast.[9] By this point, many heavily populated states were callable, including Texas, Florida, Pennsylvania, Illinois, Ohio, and Michigan. At this point, total electoral votes that then could be projected—328 in 1992–2000 and 331 for 1984–1988—already exceeded the 270 needed to win the presidency. The victor did not even have to sweep these states; the loser could be projected to carry seven northeastern states and yet still be knocked out in this early "first round" (see Figures 1.1 and 1.2).

By the second round, 6:00 P.M. PST, over 80 percent of the electoral vote could be forecast, making it even easier for the networks to call an election while voters in the West were still going to the polls. Indeed, in six of the eight projected elections, at least one network declared the winner by or at 6:00 PST.

Round three, at 7:00 P.M. PST, added few electoral votes, mostly from less populated Rocky Mountain states. To date, those states have never put any candidate over the top. In 1992, when Bill Clinton was declared the winner at 7:48, he had just been awarded Ohio.

Round four, at 8:00 P.M. PST, concludes voting in California, Oregon, Washington, and Hawaii, leaving only Alaska outstanding. Surprisingly, projections have never been issued at this hour. None of the dozen presidential elections from 1960 to 2004 was successfully projected between 8:00 and midnight PST. Either the race had already been projected or it was so extremely close that it required more hours (or weeks) to be decided.

Figure 1.3 shows the states that were eligible to be projected in

**Figure 1.1   Cumulative Electoral Votes, 1984–1988, by Hour Most
Polls Closed in Each State**

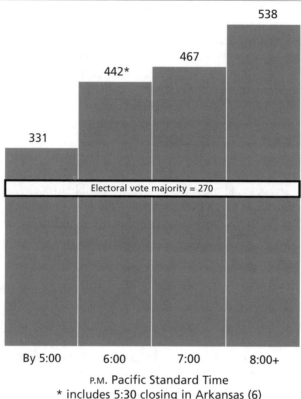

P.M. Pacific Standard Time
* includes 5:30 closing in Arkansas (6)

each of these four rounds. At first glance, it seems odd that the states in
white carried so much weight, but their impact was due to population,
not square miles. To see each state drawn in proportion to its electoral
votes, see Figure 1.4, a cartogram illustrating the eastern population
tilt. Both maps (starting with the darker shades) also show the layers of
potential exposure to projections.[10]

The Far West—Alaska, Hawaii, California, Oregon, Washington,
and northern Idaho[11]—invariably gets the most potential exposure to
projections while voting is still under way. However, if the projection
is broadcast before 7:00 P.M. PST, residents of other states can also hear
the news before their polls close.

Figure 1.2 Cumulative Electoral Votes, 1992–1996 and 2000, by Hour Most Polls Closed in Each State

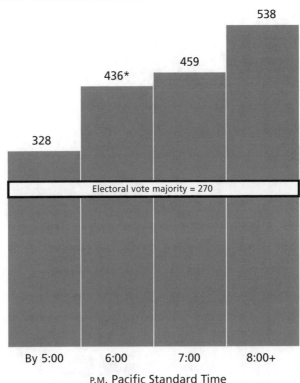

538

459

436*

328

Electoral vote majority = 270

By 5:00   6:00   7:00   8:00+

P.M. Pacific Standard Time
* includes 5:30 closing in Arkansas (6)

Projection exposure tends to decrease as one travels east, but as Figure 1.3 shows, there are exceptions. For example, Iowa keeps its polls open late (9:00 P.M. CST) and joins four Rocky Mountain states in the group that gets the second largest potential dose of projections.

When projections were aired during the 5:00 P.M. PST hour, many more states—home to roughly four out of ten citizens—still had polls open. For example, in 1984 when CBS announced the next president at 5:00 P.M. PST, potential voters in twenty-two states (and parts of three others) still had at least one hour to cast their ballots. Even the two Atlantic Coast states where polls close late—New York and Rhode Island—were subject to projections for one hour.

**Figure 1.3   Times When States Were Treated as "Projectable,"
1960–2000**

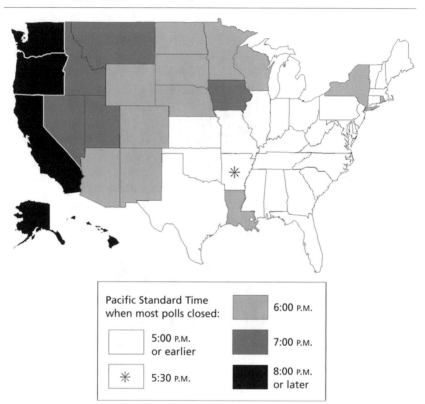

Post-2000 Adjustment

After the public outcry over the botched Florida projections in 2000, one reform was that networks promised to wait until *all* polls closed in a state before projecting that state. In congressional hearings, news division presidents pledged, in the words of ABC's David Westin, "not to project the race in any state until all of the polls, not just the substantial majority, have closed in that state."[12] Skeptics were impressed to see that the broadcast and cable news networks kept their word when covering the 2002 congressional elections and again during the hotly contested 2004 presidential election.

Not only does this change delay calling Florida until the state's western panhandle finishes voting, but it also postpones for another

Figure 1.4   Times When States Were Projectable with Size Proportionate to 1984–1988 Electoral College Vote

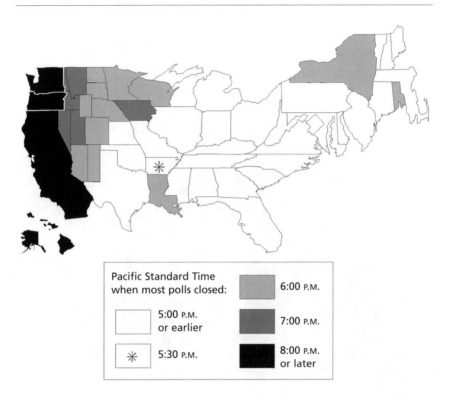

hour the earliest verdicts on Texas, Michigan, and Kansas while the networks politely wait for everyone in those asynchronous dual-zone states to finish voting. This policy shift has a noteworthy implication for projecting the winner of the race for the White House: it delays the earliest possible projection by one full hour. As shown in Figure 1.5, under this new system, only 269 electoral votes become projectable at 5:00 P.M. PST, falling short of the needed 270-vote majority. Moving the 57 electoral votes of Texas, Michigan, and Kansas and subtracting a net of 2 electoral votes due to post-2000 redistricting pushes back the projection process (see Figure 1.6). If the networks all continue to respect this new self-imposed limitation, it will reduce the duration and scope of potential exposure to early projection in future elections. As shown in Figure 1.7, ten states will possibly be subject to at least one hour of

Figure 1.5   Cumulative Electoral Votes, 2004–2008, by Hour Final Polls Close in Each State

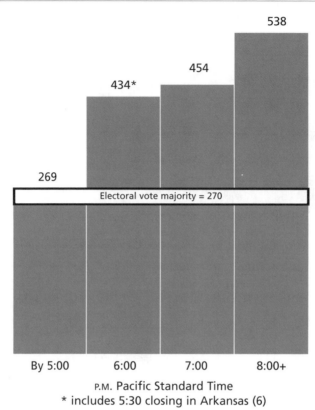

By 5:00   6:00   7:00   8:00+

P.M. Pacific Standard Time
* includes 5:30 closing in Arkansas (6)

projection news before their polls close, rather than twenty-two states and parts of three others (cf. Figure 1.3) as in the past.

While the Far West has not been the only region exposed to projections during balloting, no other region has so much exposure under either the new or the previous network practices. As a result, the controversy and research surrounding projections have centered on the West Coast. For simplicity, references in this book to those most exposed to projections are to "westerners," although that word does not precisely capture the varying levels of exposure that have sometimes reached farther east. While others may be exposed to projections from time to time, residents of the West Coast have still been the most vocal in their objections.

**Figure 1.6   Final Poll Closings by State with Size Proportionate to
2004–2008 Electoral College Vote**

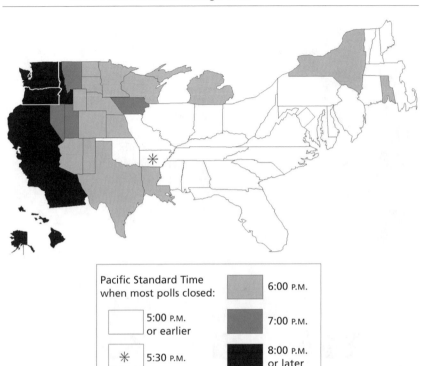

Pacific Standard Time when most polls closed:

- 5:00 P.M. or earlier
- 5:30 P.M.
- 6:00 P.M.
- 7:00 P.M.
- 8:00 P.M. or later

Framing the Debate

Projections have invariably prompted complaints, but those in 1964, 1980, 1984, and 2000 generated the most controversy, congressional hearings, and newspaper articles.[13] Hearings on Capitol Hill consisted mainly of antiprojection testimony from a series of unhappy western officials (from county clerks to U.S. representatives) and "good government" groups (such as the League of Women Voters) versus proprojection testimony from network news presidents and vice presidents.

Critics tended to frame their objections in terms of the damage to voter turnout that they believed was caused by projections. Defenders replied that those claims were based on unsubstantiated anecdotes. Moreover, they said, the issue was not turnout but freedom of speech. Thus, network representatives said the solution to any alleged turnout

Figure 1.7   Maximum Exposure to Projections When Networks Wait Until All Polls Close in Each State

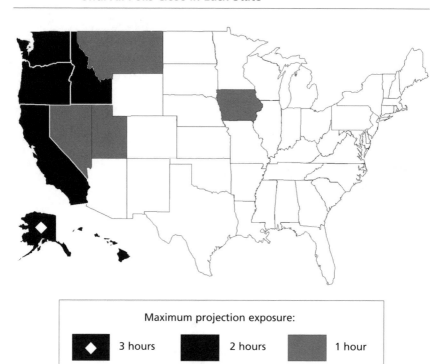

Maximum projection exposure:

◆ 3 hours   ■ 2 hours   ▨ 1 hour

problem was not for the networks voluntarily to cease issuing projections but for Congress to pass a nationwide uniform poll-closing law.

Twice in the 1980s, the House did pass bills mandating that all polls close simultaneously at 9:00 P.M. EST (except in Alaska and Hawaii), but the bills died in the Senate. The House also passed formal resolutions requesting that the networks withhold projections until the polls closed nationwide. Those resolutions were ignored, and the leading congressional opponent of projections, Al Swift (D-Wash.), lamented: "If they were polluting the air, Congress could pass a law, but when they pollute the election we're helpless because of the First Amendment" guaranteeing freedom of the press. "[Networks] hide behind the First Amendment and go, 'nah-nah-nah-nah-nah.'"[14]

Compared to the Senate, the House seemed far more hostile to projections, exacerbated perhaps by the shock of two powerful western

Democrats being narrowly defeated following network projections of a Republican takeover of the White House in 1980.[15] The notion that the networks were the culprits was fueled by unverified anecdotes about long lines of western voters walking away from the polls upon hearing that "it's all over" because Ronald Reagan had won.

Personally sensitive to the importance of turnout in close elections, politicians seemed worried about that issue above all else. The 1984 congressional report on projections illustrates this perspective. Summarizing three years of hearings and the Committee on House Administration's conclusion that projections have an "adverse impact on the election process," 80 percent of the findings are devoted to the issue of voter turnout.[16] Only 20 percent are devoted to an additional objection to projections—that they do not treat all Americans equitably or respectfully.

How a topic is framed structures its public debate. That frame sets boundaries on the way people think about and analyze the topic. In this case, critics gravitated to the more concrete issue of turnout. Consequently, they needed compelling evidence, beyond just anecdotes, to build a case based on the claim of decreased turnout. Lost in much of the debate has been the issue of fairness—perhaps because it seemed more subjective or because critics assumed that decreased turnout would be easy to demonstrate.

When academic researchers turned to the topic, they followed this same path. Studies centered on whether projections decreased voter turnout in the West. Few other possible behavioral effects were explored. Some scattered hints have suggested that projections might actually stimulate some tardy voters to get to the polls, but few researchers pursued that possibility. Three large early studies examined whether projections might motivate some people to switch their votes (via either "bandwagon" or "underdog" effects), but they found no evidence of vote switching.[17]

In regard to the issue of citizen equity, only one scholarly analysis of the fairness of projections was found, and even that discussion features the element of decreased turnout.[18] The issue of fairness did emerge strikingly in the series of focus groups summarized in Chapter 8 and considered again in Chapter 10.

While the issue of fairness is explored in these later chapters, fairness has not been, for better or worse, at the heart of the public debate. Overall, both the political and academic worlds have concentrated on the possible negative consequences of projections on voter turnout.

Since projections could plausibly cause such mischief, that focus has been reasonable. It is not the only worthwhile question about projections, but it is a provocative one that is relevant to shaping public policy as well as to understanding the mass media's complex role in U.S. politics.

Most chapters in this book revolve around the straightforward turnout hypothesis that has been at the heart of most of the public and academic controversy about projections. The hypothesis can be stated simply as:

> *Projections (the independent variable) decrease voter turnout (the dependent variable).*

The classic vision of science is that scholars are supposed to deduce hypotheses from theory for the strict purpose of testing that theory. In practice, however, hypotheses often stem from issues of applied public policy and other ad hoc matters. In this book, the central research question—whether projections decrease voter turnout—originated in the ongoing public controversy and was not deduced from theory. Nevertheless, this type of applied research can still benefit from (and perhaps contribute to) academic theory and scholarship. Before investigating the impact of projections on voter turnout, it is useful to provide some theoretical context and to fit this topic into the broader study of voter turnout. In other words: Why do people vote?

To Vote or Not to Vote

Over the years, political scientists have devoted considerable energy to trying to understand why people choose to vote. Some have found it remarkable that anyone votes at all, because the act of voting appears to lack a strictly rational explanation. The chore of voting takes some time and effort, and has an infinitesimal chance of making any difference. Anthony Downs (1957) famously framed the paradox this way: "Why does anyone bother to vote, given that voting is presumably costly and that the probability that one's vote will affect the outcome is presumably small?"[19]

Other political scientists have reversed the emphasis to ask: "Why do so many people *not* vote?" Why is voter turnout in the United States not higher? Why has turnout declined since 1960? Michael McDonald and Samuel Popkin (2001) found that, contrary to conventional wisdom, turnout did *not* continue to drop after the mid-1970s. Their explanation is a simple one: the most widely cited percentages—turnout of the *voting-age* population—fail to exclude ineligible adults such as immigrants, legal and otherwise. Increasing immigration has meant increasing numbers of ineligible adults in the voting-age pool, thereby pushing turnout rates artificially downward.

Figure 1.8 shows national trends calculated using both voting-age population and voting-*eligible* population, which excludes immigrants, felons, and others ineligible to register and vote. Contrary to reports based on voting-age data, since the 1972 plunge, turnout among voting-eligible Americans has not been sliding steadily downward.

Even if turnout was higher than commonly supposed for most of three decades, researchers are still challenged to explain why participation rates failed to *increase* after 1960. Three major changes ought to have pushed turnout firmly higher:

1. Americans became more affluent and better educated, and affluent, educated citizens have higher turnout rates.

Figure 1.8   Voter Turnout Trends Based on Voting-Age vs. Voting-Eligible Population

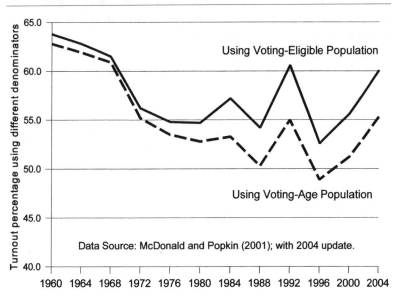

2. Voter registration became much easier, including simpler registration procedures, shorter residency requirements, less stringent purging of the names of those who fail to vote, and shorter registration deadlines.
3. Poll taxes, literacy tests, and other voting barriers to blacks in the South were eliminated.

In the 1960s and 1970s, voter turnout did soar in the Deep South as millions of African Americans increasingly exercised the franchise they had often been denied. That transformation was unmistakable. Yet this success adds to the puzzle of why—in the face of more education, greater affluence, and easier registration—national turnout rates failed to increase steadily over the ensuing decades. What contrary pressures have been at work? Or to pose the question comprehensively: What factors stimulate or depress voter turnout in the United States?

Possible Predictors of Turnout

Many turnout influences have been suggested in numerous books and articles. Naturally, academic researchers have been drawn to factors most closely aligned with their fields—sociologists to the dominion of groups, scholars of mass communications to the news media's role, economists to rent-seeking and other cost-benefit issues, political scientists to more overtly political elements. From these and other perspectives, many causes have been proposed.

Fifty variables that various scholars have suggested as influencing the likelihood of voting are summarized in Figure 1.9. This list is not exhaustive but it does include most factors that have been documented or at least seriously proposed as influential. Along with a few illustrative citations, the fifty factors are grouped for convenience into eleven categories:

1. Some analysts have noted broad *systemic elements,* such as the possibly interest-sapping structure that offers only two parties and no proportional representation (Jackman, 1987), along with the high frequency of national, state, and local primary, general, and special elections (Boyd, 1989).
2. Others have studied regulations and *legal constraints* that make registration and voting inconvenient (Timpone, 1998). While such rules have been dramatically relaxed, they have not been eliminated.

3. *Demographic variables,* especially education, denote sociocultural contexts that can influence voter participation (Wolfinger and Rosenstone, 1980). Turnout also varies markedly by generation, with World War II's "greatest generation" having the highest turnout of all (Miller, 1992; Lyons and Alexander, 2000).

4. Involvement with *social networks* raises another array of plausible influences on voting. Under this umbrella are interpersonal connections and being rooted in a community (Teixera, 1992), political conversations in those networks (Straits, 1991; Lucas and Adams, 1978), and being married (Straits, 1990), all of which are associated with higher turnout.

5. Some voters may be guided by specific *instrumental factors.* "Rent-seeking" goals appear to motivate voting among many public schoolteachers, farmers, and others whose livelihood directly depends heavily or entirely on government policies (Wolfinger and Rosenstone, 1980). Perhaps a few people even skip registration to avoid jury duty (Oliver and Wolfinger, 1999).

6. Turnout is also related to *long-term political orientations,* especially intensity of party loyalty, beliefs about government responsiveness (Abramson and Aldrich, 1982), alienation (Southwell and Everest, 1998), and political cynicism (Teixeira, 1992).

7. More short-term *campaign-specific political reactions* may also turn off or turn on potential voters, especially the extent to which a candidate is perceived as appealing or appalling (Zipp, 1985) but including other factors such as interest in initiatives and referenda (Tolbert, Grummel, and Smith, 2001).

8. *Long-term media themes* constitutes another category that has been proposed as influencing voter turnout. For example, Thomas Patterson (2002) argues that news coverage tends to suffocate citizens' participatory zeal through years of relentlessly negative "attack journalism" (see also Robinson, 1976).

9. For a specific election, the *media construction of the campaign* may energize or discourage participation—depending on how individuals process those media messages (Graber, 1988)—as they react to campaign news (Kennamer, 1987), campaign advertisements, including negative ads (Lau et al., 1999; Ansolabehere and Iyengar, 1995), and televised debates, among other things.

10. Various *election-day pressures* may impact potential voters, including vigorous get-out-the-vote efforts (Adams and Smith, 1980; Wielhouwer, 1994, 2000). Although usually ignored in academic stud-

ies, the election-day obstacles most commonly mentioned by nonvoters are obligations at home or at work, as well as problems with transportation, weather, and health (Schur and Kruse, 2000; see also Table 4.2).

11. A final possible category of influences is the *perceived competitiveness* of the election—both prior to election day and conceivably on election day when the networks project the winner of the White House while ballots are still being cast in some states.

This compiled list of potential influences could probably be expanded, contracted, and reorganized indefinitely. Its role here is to suggest the enormous range of factors that scholars have proposed as contributing to the likelihood of voting or not voting.

Figure 1.9   Fifty Factors Suggested as Influencing Voter Turnout

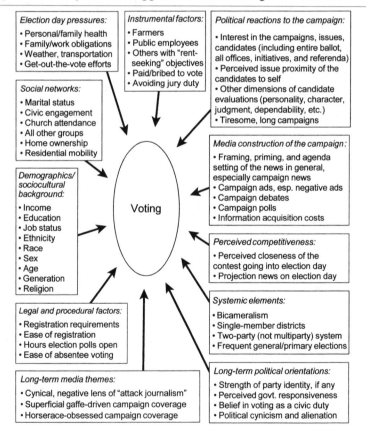

A Multilevel Model of Turnout

Widely differing degrees of empirical support have been found for these fifty factors, a few of which are little more than grand speculations. Rather than a cluttered model with dozens of variables, scholars customarily try to isolate a few powerful predictors. While they may spar over which factors are strongest, all of these elements could have at least some direct or indirect influence on the decision to vote. No two are necessarily mutually exclusive. This daunting assortment of possible influences—systemic, structural, political, sociological, psychological, economic, and even medical—can be all accommodated in a single elaborate model of turnout. Figure 1.10 illustrates the major links in one possible model that integrates all eleven sets of factors.[20]

At the start of this model are permanent or usually long-term factors that would contribute to underlying political orientations that may directly influence the propensity to vote and may also stimulate media attentiveness (probably a two-way process, as news may reinforce or undercut those underlying perspectives). Other than social networks, shown with an unmediated link to turnout, mass media become the primary vehicle for information acquisition, evaluations of candidates and issues through the priming and framing of political events, and influencing interest in electoral participation. Of course, mass media messages would still undergo the crucial step of being processed (interpreted and reinterpreted) by potential voters.

The model also posits legal constraints and election day pressures (such as illness) as independent influences on voting, although individual commitment (based on the previous factors) would probably affect whether a headache or shorter voting hours would be seen as insurmountable.

The purpose of this model is to suggest some reasonable relationships to help locate network projections amid the multitude of factors that may influence voter turnout. There is immense competition for influence, but thanks to the clock, the location of projections in any proposed model of turnout is easy to position as one of the last possible elements in this vast "funnel of causality."

Despite the complexity of forces shaping participation, the model actually becomes less complex in the waning hours of the last day of the campaign. In states where polls are open, people who are eligible to vote but have not yet done so already have a propensity to vote or not to vote if and when they hear projections. Myriad influences are already in

Figure 1.10 Model of Factors Potentially Influencing Voter Turnout

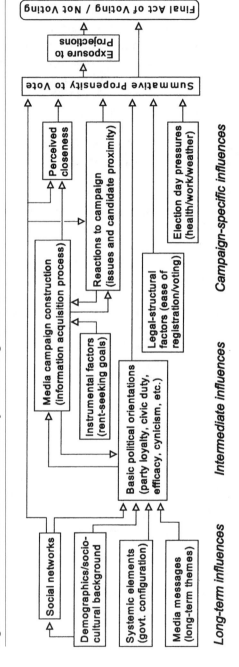

place—from childhood civics lessons to that final campaign commercial heard on the radio. The cumulative force of these countless pressures has already shaped an inclination to vote or not to vote prior to the moment of exposure to projection news.

If the preexisting likelihood of voting is conceptualized as ranging from certainty (1.0) to impossibility (0.0), those near 0.5, teetering between voting and not voting, should be the most vulnerable to projections (see Figure 1.11). A few words broadcast from New York should not derail those whose cumulative lifelong pressures are strongly propelling them to vote. On the other hand, projection news might conceivably be a pivotal last blow that would deter at least some cross-pressured, ambivalent potential voters. How often that last-minute deflection occurs determines the extent to which projections lower voter turnout, if at all. Such occurrences, the voting literature suggests, are likely to be severely circumscribed—but not necessarily eliminated—by a legion of lifelong influences.

Summary

Television networks have often been able to project the next president quite rapidly by taking advantage of exit polls and the electoral vote concentration in the eastern and central time zones. Even under a new policy of waiting until all the polls close in each state, the networks can

Figure 1.11   Isolating Potential Projection Effects

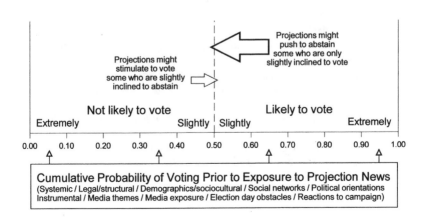

still potentially declare the victor as early as two hours before West Coast polls close.

Projections spark a recurring controversy centering on the claim that voter turnout is damaged by these early verdicts. Indeed, both politicians and professors have focused on turnout rather than on the issue of fairness. Following in that vein, research presented in this book mainly targets the dispute over voter turnout, but does return to the important issue of equity in later chapters.

The decision to vote, scholars have suggested, hinges on a wide variety of long-term and short-term influences, including family, friends, society, media, candidates, parties, laws, and other factors. Faced with so many preexisting pressures, are people pushed away from the polls by projections? To measure the distinct impact of projections, varied methodologies were employed for this book. A different approach in a different location is presented in each chapter: surveys in Portland, a time series in Los Angeles, county comparisons in Kansas and Idaho, a natural experiment in eastern Oregon, an eclectic approach for the Florida panhandle, and focus groups in San Diego, Seattle, and elsewhere. These diverse efforts were built on lessons learned from previous studies of projections, the topic of the next chapter.

Notes

1. Secretary of State Ralph Munro of Washington, quoted in "Western Leaders Push Uniform Poll-Closing Time," *Seattle Times,* November 14, 1988. Munro added, "The equal system of voting in America is gone as long as this takes place."

2. Ibid. Governor Neil Goldschmidt of Oregon: "Our elections . . . are too important to be decided at network headquarters."

3. Ibid. Governor Booth Gardner of Washington: "It says to them 'your vote doesn't count.' . . . It diminishes the value of our right to vote."

4. California Republican leader John Herrington, quoted in Howard Kurtz, "GOP Blasts Networks' Plan to Name Victor," *Washington Post,* October 30, 1996.

5. R. McLeod, "Poll Closing Law Urged," *San Francisco Chronicle,* November 10, 1988.

6. Calling states using exit-poll data alone, without actual votes, is a practice that was begun by NBC in 1980 (see Chapter 3).

7. Definitive information on state election practices has been difficult to obtain. Seemingly authoritative sources have had conflicting information. Conversations with state election administrators and with county election offi-

cials have been necessary to try to resolve discrepancies. In addition, actual practices do not always go as far as the law allows; state law may allow counties to keep their polls open as late as 8:00, but in practice they may close at 7:00 or earlier.

8. Three states with two time zones (Tennessee, Nebraska, South Dakota) avoided two-stage closings by ending voting at the same moment statewide (e.g., 8:00 in Nebraska's CST counties and 7:00 in its MST counties). In practice, voting in Alaska usually finishes by 8:00 Alaska time because the handful of precincts in the far western tail of the Aleutian Islands (on Hawaii-Aleutian time) either close early or vote absentee. In Oregon, only one rural county was in its MST zone, so the networks always waited until polls closed in the PST rest of the state. In New Hampshire, most cities have used their option of closing at 8:00 rather than 7:00 as required of townships; networks have projected the state using the earlier time. The networks' treatment of North Dakota has varied and even state officials have not always had current information about exactly when polls closed in each country. For more on North Dakota practices, see Chapter 6.

9. Most times reported in this book are Pacific standard time—not eastern (TV network headquarters time). The default is PST because that time zone has the most people who get the most exposure to projections. Hawaii, despite being two time zones farther west, can be added to the West Coast group because its polls close at 6:00 Hawaii time (8:00 PST). Daylight saving time has ended the last Sunday in October and has not impinged on November elections.

10. Exceptions are northern PST Idaho, the El Paso MST western tip of Texas, and a far western row of counties in MST Kansas and in CST Michigan. Thus, for example, Texas was "callable" at 5:00 PST, although El Paso polls were open another hour.

11. Northern Idaho is in the Pacific Time Zone and its polls stay open until 8:00 PST, along with those of Pacific Coast states. However, using their "most polls closed" shortcut, the networks treated Idaho as projectable when polls closed at 8:00 MST in southern Idaho, where a majority of the state's population lives.

12. "Election Night Coverage by the Networks," Committee on Energy and Commerce, U.S. House of Representatives, 117th Congress, 1st session, no. 107-25 (Washington, D.C.: U.S. Government Printing Office, 2001), p. 97. CBS did not make the same pledge at that time, but all the networks followed this important new policy in reporting the 2002 and 2004 elections.

13. In 1964, CBS sparked a tempest by announcing that conservative Barry Goldwater had won the crucial California Republican primary when ballots could still be cast for another thirty-eight minutes in northern California. This was no ordinary primary either; Goldwater narrowly defeated liberal Nelson Rockefeller by 51 to 49 percent, clinching the GOP nomination and launching the conservative conquest of the party. (Some see the 1964 CBS statement as the first unequivocal projection; those in 1960 were more tentative.) "Man on the Bandwagon," *Time,* June 12, 1964. In 1980 and 1984, the

heavily Democratic U.S. House of Representatives was incensed by the very early projections of Republican Ronald Reagan's victories. In 2000, unjustified projections of the pivotal state of Florida, in the evening and again in the morning, also provoked outrage.

14. U.S. Representative Al Swift (D-Wash.), quoted in "Network Exit Polls Blasted in State," *Seattle Times,* November 7, 1984.

15. The two defeated representatives were Al Ullman of Oregon and James Corman of California. Ullman chaired the powerful House Ways and Means Committee and Corman chaired, of all things, the Democratic Congressional Campaign Committee.

16. Committee on House Administration, report no. 98-671, 98th Congress, 2nd session of the U.S. House of Representatives.

17. Three major studies interviewed thousands of voters immediately before and after the election. None found any hint that projections had influenced final candidate choices. Kurt Lang and Gladys Lang said "not a single late voter in either state reported having switched from one candidate to another" for president or for senator (1968, p. 97). Harold Mendelsohn (1966) contrasted prevote intentions with the reported vote of those exposed to landslide news and found no evidence of either bandwagon or underdog effects. Likewise, Douglas Fuchs (1966) uncovered no significant evidence of vote switching.

18. Thompson, 2002, pp. 98–105.

19. Downs's question—"Why does anyone bother to vote?"—is one that some academics have sought to answer using models of rational political behavior based on tangible measures of costs and benefits. This approach, called "rational choice," "political economics," or "public choice," sometimes predicts political behavior rather well, but to explain voting it has been necessary to go beyond concrete costs and benefits and introduce cultural/psychological factors such as psychic gratification from doing one's civic duty (Riker and Ordeshook, 1968). If many people vote because they consider it a duty, then the decision to participate is not just a matter of rational actors weighing the remote benefit that they might personally decide the outcome of the election.

20. A more complex model might be constructed as a two-stage process, with the first part building toward voter registration and the second part to voting, since somewhat different dynamics affect each stage (Jackson, 1996).

2

Reassessing
Conflicting
Findings

What have previous studies discovered about the impact of early projections on voter turnout? Findings have varied greatly—from no effects to minuscule effects to large effects. Some analysts have attributed these diverse findings to inadequate methodologies. One review of the literature came to these harsh conclusions:

> The labels of absent, inconclusive, and inconsistent provide fitting descriptions for the evidence. . . . Too much is indirect and obliquely related to the issue at hand, not robust enough or reliable enough, and not internally consistent.
>
> Given the relative crudeness and insensitivity of the overall methodology employed, it is perhaps no surprise that most of the reported studies were not quite up to the task.[1]

However "inconclusive and inconsistent" prior studies may be, they still offer a valuable resource. Methodological problems that they faced may yield insights that can be exploited in the trial-and-error process of social research. Moreover, perhaps additional lessons can be learned by discovering why the results of these studies varied so much. To achieve these goals, prior research was reviewed using the conventions of meta-analysis.

Meta-Analysis Methods

Meta-analysis is a methodology for systematically gathering and analyzing prior research. The initial step is to search for relevant studies in a replicable way and offer a transparent, thorough account of that process. Next the assembled studies are reviewed and coded in an orderly fashion; key elements of the context and methods of each are recorded. The statistical findings of each study, which may be based on different measures, are usually converted into a standardized measure of "effects size." When those findings vary markedly, meta-analysts can search for patterns among factors that might possibly account for the divergent outcomes, especially different settings or different methodologies.[2]

Five large full-text databases were searched from their earliest available date (in one case 1906) through June 2003.[3] These databases encompassed leading journals of public opinion, mass communication, and political science, as well as many other academic publications. Relevant articles from the database search were then combed for references to other studies; this "snowball" process was repeated until no new studies were found in their citations.

To be included, published scholarly studies had to present new research meeting three criteria: (1) be a data-based analysis (using any research design) examining the impact of (2) network projections of the winning presidential candidate on (3) voter turnout (no matter how it was measured).[4] Articles that discussed only previous academic studies or lacked data on nonvoters were excluded.[5]

These search and screening procedures yielded only eleven publications. Just in case the search terms (listed in endnote 3) had failed to catch all relevant studies, a nonelectronic search was conducted, involving a manual inspection of the tables of contents of all 1990–2002 issues of *Public Opinion Quarterly, American Political Science Review, American Politics Quarterly, Journalism and Mass Communication Quarterly,* and *Journal of Broadcasting and Electronic Media.* This search did not locate any additional studies.

A final tactic was to exploit three major reports that were prepared following the projection problems that plagued election night 2000.[6] These reports cited academic studies, but none that had not been previously identified. With that corroboration, the meta-analysis proceeded with the nine articles and two books found in the initial search.

Scholarly studies often use different measures. In that case, meta-analyses need to standardize their results ("effects size") to make consistent comparisons possible. That step was fairly simple here because these projection studies almost always reported their findings in terms of the percentage change in total voter turnout or in nonvoter turnout (which can be converted to total voter turnout) in California or all West Coast states.

Effects sizes are summarized in Table 2.1. The median finding was a decrease of 0.9 percent in total voter turnout in one or more western states, but the deviation around that midpoint is considerable: one study found a large positive effect, four detected little or no effects, one measured small but less trivial negative effects, and five calculated moderate to large negative effects.

Any result suggesting that projections cause 1 out of every 20 eligible citizens to fail to vote (i.e., –5.0 percent) is certainly a large effect, while turning away 1 in 1,000 (i.e., –0.1 percent) can fairly be described

Table 2.1 Effects Summary

	Largest Impact on Total Voter Turnout in One or More Western States	Data Type
Large positive		
Epstein and Strom (1981)	+7.0	Aggregate
None or trivial negative		
Mendelsohn (1966)	0.0	Survey
Fuchs (1966)	0.0	Survey
Lang and Lang (1968)	–0.1	Survey
Epstein and Strom (1984)	–0.2	Survey
Small negative		
Tannenbaum and Kostrich (1983, p. 60)	–0.9	Survey
Moderate to large negative		
Wolfinger and Linquiti (1981)	–2.7	Comparative survey
Dubois (1983)	–3.6	Aggregate
Delli Carpini (1984)	–5.6	Aggregate
Sudman (1986)	–6.0	Aggregate
Jackson (1983)	–6.0 (–3.0 to –12.0?)[a]	Comparative survey

Notes: a. Scholars have not agreed on how Jackson's equations convert to a specific percentage decrease in turnout. See endnote 19.

as a very small effect. Regardless of the adjective used, these varied estimates can hardly be described as a consensus.

When findings are so disparate, meta-analysts often examine patterns that might explain why results diverged. Here, the review begins with the aggregate studies, which, as shown in Table 2.1, showed much more variation than did standard surveys.

Aggregate Data Studies

Four studies were built on aggregate data using total votes cast in districts or states instead of individual survey interviews. Two studies made state and regional comparisons for 1960–1980 (Epstein and Strom, 1981; Dubois 1983), while two compared estimated turnout in congressional districts in the projected 1980 election against a turnout average from nonprojected years (Delli Carpini, 1984; Sudman, 1986). As shown in Table 2.1, three of these four studies found a large turnout decline in western states in the projected election of 1980. The fourth (Epstein and Strom), however, reached the opposite conclusion.

How did these studies arrive at such conflicting results regarding the same election? They used very different measures of voter turnout. Epstein and Strom calculated turnout as a percentage of the estimated *voting-age population,* while the other three studies calculated turnout as a percentage of *registered voters* (that is, the total number of names on voter registration lists).

One might end the scrutiny of these inconsistent findings at this point. However, additional probing of the data was prompted by Seymour Sudman's puzzling comment that the large relationship he found was due entirely to California: "[With] so many districts California dominates these results. If California were excluded there would be no differences between the remaining states where the polls closed late and the other states where they closed early" (1986, pp. 337–338).

That was a strange finding. It does not seem reasonable that Californians were hypersensitive to projections at the very same time Oregonians, Washingtonians, Alaskans, and Hawaiians were immune. Closer investigation revealed that Californians themselves were not so odd. It was the California registration data that were odd, a classic problem of "instrumentation" (changes in the way something is measured) that damaged three of these four aggregate studies.

Before 1978, California used a stringent system intended to delete the names of everyone who did not vote in the prior election. Indeed, millions of voters were removed from the rolls after three low-turnout elections, in 1972, 1973, and 1974.[7] Then, in 1978, California radically transformed its registration record-keeping by halting its automatic purging of nonvoters. Millions of nonvoters stayed on the rolls after the 1978 election, giving 1980 registration drives a tremendous head start. Right on cue, registration numbers in 1980 began to bulk up after seven lean years (see Figure 2.1).

These extraordinary changes destroyed any time series based on the turnout of "registered voters." California's automatic purging had

Figure 2.1 California Population, Voting-Eligible Population, and Registered Voters, 1970–1982

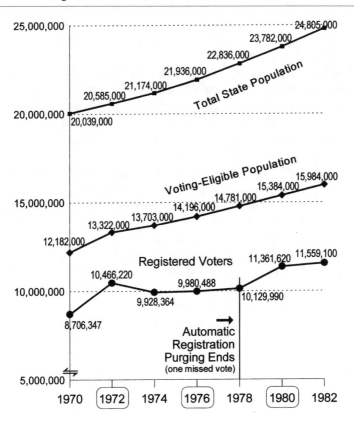

deeply deflated voter registration lists in 1972–1974 and made turnout of registered voters in 1976 (an unprojected election) look higher. After automatic purging ended, the lists became more inflated with the names of people who were less participatory or had moved or died, thus making turnout among registered voters in 1980 look lower—for reasons that had nothing to do with projections.

Without this misleading California time series, what remains of the three aggregate studies that found large negative projection effects? Without California, Sudman found no effects at all. Removing California from Delli Carpini's study shrinks turnout effects in the West to –0.8 percent.[8] And Phillip Dubois's study, which relied entirely on California registration data, now has to be omitted.

Unchanged is Laurily Epstein and Gerald Strom's time series, which used California's estimated voting-age population, not its shifting voter registration lists. They found no evidence that projections depressed turnout. To the contrary, the downward trend in turnout nearly ended in the projected election of 1980, although they noted that many factors could be responsible.

All four aggregate studies represent ambitious efforts to compare turnout differences in projected and unprojected elections between western (mainly California) and other states. The researchers faced two colossal problems—obtaining reliable data and ruling out alternative explanations. Both issues offer lessons that can help guide future research:

1. *Turnout is extremely difficult to measure consistently over the years and across jurisdictions.* Obtaining valid, reliable data in social research is a never-ending challenge, and measuring voter turnout is no exception. These studies calculated turnout rates as a percentage of either the total number of names recorded on voter registration lists or the estimated voting-age population. Unfortunately, both methods have serious shortcomings when the goal is to detect minute variations in turnout.

Voter registration lists do offer the appearance of precision, with a firm count (not an estimate) of the exact number of names on official rolls. Their flaw, as the California case vividly illustrates, is that the laws and practices of registration record-keeping—and the ensuing amount of inflation in the lists—change over time and differ between jurisdictions.

The alternative of using the estimated voting-age population (or the estimated voting-eligible population) to figure turnout rates is also less than precise.[9] Those estimates get progressively less reliable every year that passes after the prior census.[10] After the 2000 census, the United States was discovered to have 2.5 percent more residents than the Census Bureau had estimated—with discrepancies varying markedly among states. Retrospective "intercensal estimates" use the newest census to recalculate all the "postcensal estimates" (especially improving the end-of-decade estimates); the Census Bureau (1990, p. 36) has called this "an attempt to introduce increasingly accurate data" but still does not recommend drawing conclusions based on small differences even with improved intercensal estimates. As for using these estimates to calculate voter turnout, the Census Bureau has urged caution, concluding (in rare italics) that "*small differences in voter participation should not be accorded great substantive significance*" (1990, p. 36).

2. *Even if aggregate data were more precise, turnout differences between elections and states cannot all be attributed to projections when so many other factors could also cause changes in turnout.* With or without projections, turnout will surely vary between western and other states from one election to the next. Political dynamics do not evolve in perfect symmetry across the nation. Variations in turnout could be due to differences in the appeal of candidates and their issues, the weather, get-out-the-vote efforts, controversial ballot initiatives, the presence or absence of a U.S. Senate race, the composition of the electorate, social trends, and many other factors.[11]

Survey-Based Studies

The seven remaining studies all used data from postelection surveys of voters and nonvoters. Again, results varied considerably depending on the methodology that was used. The weakest effects (0.0 to –0.9 percent) were found in the five studies that reported the percentage of nonvoters (eligible to vote) who told interviewers that projections (more or less) were the reason they had not voted (see Table 2.2).

These five "standard" surveys made important contributions. The earliest ones documented that a sizable share of late-day voters had heard projections and were undaunted. While that may seem obvious in retrospect, it was not so obvious at the time. Also, while some people feared that projections would cause bandwagon or underdog effects, large pre- and postelection surveys of voters found no signs of vote switching.[12]

Table 2.2   Effects Summary for Survey-Based Studies

	Largest Effect Found on Total Voter Turnout in the West
Studies reporting the percentage of nonvoters eligible to vote who blamed projections	
Mendelsohn (1966)	0
Fuchs (1966)	0
Lang and Lang (1968)	–0.1
Epstein and Strom (1984)	–0.2
Kostrich and Tannenbaum (1983, p. 60)	–0.9
Other survey-based studies	
Wolfinger and Linquiti (1981)	–2.7
Jackson (1983)	–6.0 (–3 to –12?)

Few nonvoters in these five surveys cited projections as their reason for not voting. While the onus for nonvoting could easily have been put on the networks, remarkably few individuals did so. In all five surveys combined, out of 654 nonvoters eligible to vote, only 12 people blamed the networks. That represents 1.8 percent of the nonvoters, which, if a common pattern holds, would represent only about one-fifth to one-fourth of 1 percent of the valid eligible electorate.

These five surveys did not complete interviews with more nonvoters because they encountered two startling problems:

1. *Once invalid names were culled from registration lists, the actual turnout of valid registered voters was far higher than expected, leaving a much smaller pool of nonvoters eligible to vote.* Voter registration rolls were so inflated that Douglas Fuchs (1966), Kurt Lang and Gladys Lang (1968), and others found that as many as three-fourths of the "nonvoters" on voter registration lists had moved or died.[13] When confined to those living in their registered precinct on presidential election days, true turnout of registered voters has been high. Often, about nine out of ten valid registered voters vote in presidential elections.[14] (When deploring low turnout in the United States, journalists reasonably point to the low turnout of the entire voting-age population, not the high turnout among valid registered voters.)

2. *Many nonvoters are reluctant to admit they did not vote.* While this came as no surprise, the problem's magnitude did. For example, John Jackson's survey (1981) suffered a loss of 30 percent of its verified nonvoters because they claimed to have voted, and other surveys lost even more. Out of 1,700 registered California voters, Harold Mendelsohn (1966) found only 26 admitted nonvoters.

These two complications made it difficult to track down very many valid registered voters who did not vote and were willing to admit it. To make the challenge greater, interviews need to be conducted as soon as possible to obtain accurate recollections. If asked two months later, how well can most people really recall the exact time that things were heard and done on election day?[15]

Two Outlier Surveys

The two studies that used survey data in more creative analyses (Jackson, 1983; Wolfinger and Linquiti, 1981) obtained far larger effects, from –2.7 percent to as much as –12 percent depending on the interpretation of John Jackson's equations.

Jackson did not merely count the number of nonvoters who blamed projections.[16] Instead, he calculated the likelihood that late-day voting was less frequent among those who recalled hearing about both Jimmy Carter's early concession and the network projections. Scholars have not agreed on how to convert Jackson's probability equations to a percentage change in western turnout, but interpretations have ranged from –3 percent to as much as –12 percent.[17]

Jackson's report was popular when presented at congressional hearings, but the methodology has been criticized by Percy Tannenbaum and Leslie Kostrich (1983), Laurily Epstein and Gerald Strom (1984), and Seymour Sudman (1986). They were skeptical due to a two-month lapse between the election and the interviews,[18] along with the admittedly nonrandom and unrepresentative respondents.[19] They noted that many states were assigned to incorrect time zones.[20] Voting was erroneously assumed to end at 8:00 P.M. in all fifty states.[21] And 6:00 P.M. EST was used as the dividing point, although projections did not begin until 8:15 P.M. EST.[22]

Troubled by Jackson's computations, Epstein and Strom (1984) took the same dataset and performed a far simpler analysis. They identified 399 admitted nonvoters who said they were registered to vote. When asked why they had not voted, only 4 of them gave answers that might be linked to projections (namely, "Carter was already losing").[23]

The second outlier, also with a unique methodology, is Raymond Wolfinger and Peter Linquiti's study (1981), which used the Census Bureau's huge Current Population Surveys (CPS).[24] In 1972 and 1974, respondents were asked if and when they voted, but not whether they were exposed to projections. So, Wolfinger and Linquiti investigated whether potential exposure to projections correlated with fewer late-day voters. They found that proportionately fewer westerners than non-westerners voted late in the day in the projected 1972 election than did in the 1974 projection-free, nonpresidential election. The difference amounted to 2.7 percent fewer western voters in the projected election.

Analytically, this comparison raises the same issue noted earlier when comparing the aggregate turnout of two elections. If turnout, even late-day turnout, is lower in one projected election than it is in one unprojected election, the difference is not necessarily due to projections.[25] Wolfinger and Linquitti also had to use a low-turnout, off-year election as the unprojected election. However, strong evidence presented in Chapter 7 indicates that hourly turnout patterns in California's off-year elections have regularly diverged from those in presidential elections, with or without projections.

Summary and Future Research

Eleven published academic studies of projection effects were located for this meta-analysis. Their diverse findings ranged from no effects to large effects on voter turnout. The more straightforward studies—conventional surveys that asked nonvoters why they had not voted—consistently obtained a similar outcome: very few or no nonvoters blamed projections. In other types of studies, much of the variation in results could be attributed to flawed data (California's revamped registration records) or doubtful assumptions (treating projections as the only explanation for changes in East-West turnout).

Results of this meta-analysis thus suggest that any effects of projections on voter turnout are more likely to be small and subtle than large and pronounced. However, small effects are not the same as trivial or inconsequential effects. If projections decrease total turnout by just 1 percent, for example, that could mean the loss of roughly 3,000 votes in a single congressional district.

Convincingly measuring small effects is a challenge, but the lessons from prior research have suggested new directions. At the micro level, surveys need to rapidly and successfully interview more known nonvoters; at the macro level, comparisons need to be more closely matched and use better data. Research reported in the remainder of this book has been designed to apply these lessons in a series of original studies covering various states over numerous elections.

Despite the design and data challenges, the central question is still a modest one, concentrating on one independent variable—network projections—and its impact on one dependent variable—voter turnout. If the chapters that follow advance the understanding of that relationship, it is because they have been built on the contributions of these previous studies and their explorations of this uncharted territory.

Notes

1. Tannenbaum and Kostrich, 1983, pp. 75, 83. Their review covers a large majority of the published studies on this topic.

2. For more about meta-analysis methods, see Wilson and Lipsey, 2000; Rosenthal, 1991; and Hunter and Schmidt, 1995. Two meta-analyses related to political communication are Lau et al., 1999, on experimental tests of negative political advertising; and Glynn, Hayes, and Shanahan, 1997, which presents studies of the "spiral of silence."

3. ABI/INFORM, FirstSearch, JSTOR, PAIS (Public Affairs Information Service), and ProQuest General Reference (Periodical Abstracts). Earliest available search dates varied by journal and database (often in the 1980s); JSTOR includes every issue of its journals (e.g., *American Political Science Review* since 1906; *Public Opinion Quarterly* since 1937). The following search terms were used: *exit poll(s), election night, projections* (and) *election(s), turnout* (and) *voter.* Some major international outlets, such as the *International Journal of Public Opinion Research,* are published in English, and on this narrowly U.S. topic it is unlikely that studies were missed by not searching journals in other languages. For one study that was reported twice, Harold Mendelsohn's article (1966) was used rather than Mendelsohn and Irving Crespi's broader book (1970).

4. When feasible, the inclusion of unpublished research is often advisable due to concern that studies may be less likely to be published if they lack statistically significant results or are not "politically correct." In this case, the de-

cision was made to confine the meta-analysis to published studies both because "limited effects" studies did get published and because, despite repeated efforts, only one of four known, possibly relevant, academic, unpublished papers was successfully obtained.

5. For example, excluded was the article by Douglas Fuchs (1965) reporting interviews that were confined to late-day voters only. Included was a book by Tannenbaum and Kostrich (1983) that was largely devoted to evaluating prior research and policy options, but did offer an original scholarly analysis of the Field Institute's January 1981 California poll of both nonvoters and voters; that portion of the book was added to the meta-analysis.

6. Coauthors of these extensive reports included leading scholars, and their work provided a useful additional check. The CBS study was prepared by Linda Mason, Kathleen Frankovic, and Kathleen Hall Jamieson (2001); CNN's was by Joan Konner, James Risser, and Ben Wattenberg (2001). No previously undiscovered studies were cited in their reports or in the report of the National Commission on Federal Election Reform (2001).

7. Throughout the twentieth century, the total number of Californians registered to vote increased relentlessly, along with the state's booming population, from one presidential election to the next—with the curious exception of 1976. Why? In the 1972 election, turnout among the 10.5 million registered voters fell dramatically, automatically removing about 2 million people from the rolls. Dismal turnout in a rare statewide special election in 1973 shrank the rolls even further. Then, in the 1974 off-year election, millions of Americans, including Californians, sickened by Watergate and weary of politics, stayed home and did not vote. Despite having shed so many marginal participants in 1972 and 1973, turnout in 1974 among the culled remaining names still plunged, as more than one-third failed to vote, thereby erasing even more names. Following all this purging, voter registration drives in 1976 were unable to surpass the 1972 registration total. These developments matter because subtracting marginal participants made the 1976 turnout of registered voters (calculated based on the streamlined registration lists) appear much higher than it would have been otherwise. (In 1972, residency requirements were reduced and eighteen- to twenty-year-olds were allowed to vote, but those factors did not offset the subsequent effects of automatic purging.)

8. Michael Delli Carpini (1984) took the fresh approach of analyzing congressional districts (where changes in turnout could alter the outcome of races for the U.S. House). Seymour Sudman (1986) used Delli Carpini's innovations as the model for his own comparisons. Because exact figures were unavailable, Sudman and Delli Carpini had to calculate turnout as votes cast in each district divided by the *mean* district voter registration (the statewide total of registered voters divided by the number of districts), not by the actual number of registered voters in each district. This is problematic since levels of voter registration vary markedly from district to district, especially by the end of the decade (e.g., 1980) in growing western states before redistricting based on the new

census. Delli Carpini did offer some important caveats: "Because we are working with such small differences in numbers, many other things could be affecting the patterns we have uncovered. It is possible, that the Republicans were simply [more successful in the West that year]. Perhaps, Carter's early concession . . . was a critical magnifier of the [projection] impact. It may be that had we chosen a different method of estimation, a somewhat different pattern of impacts would have resulted" (1984, p. 882).

9. Estimates of the voting-eligible population exclude immigrants and others ineligible to vote. This may be an improvement, but it requires subtracting between-census estimates of ineligibles from between-census estimates of the voting-age population and thus compounds the need for caution when attempting to measure small turnout differences between states and between elections.

10. The Census Bureau's initial 1980 estimates of voting-age populations in the fifty states, when compared with the data later released from the actual 1980 census, show sizable gaps. The voting-age population had been underestimated by more than 4 percent in a dozen states, including Nevada by 13 percent, Florida by 10 percent, and Texas and the Carolinas by over 5 percent. Plains and Upper Midwest states had been overestimated.

11. One improvement over comparing two years (e.g., 1980 vs. 1976 turnout) is to compare a projected election with a baseline of several other elections (e.g., 1968–1972–1976). This approach (used by Sudman and Delli Carpini) still does not entirely eliminate idiosyncrasies from the baseline and does nothing to eliminate idiosyncrasies of the 1980 election, such as Jimmy Carter being less popular in western states. Dubois subtitled his article "A Note on the Hazards of Aggregate Data Analysis," pointing out that U.S. states have immense differences, elections differ greatly from year to year, and statewide totals lack data on whether individual voters and nonvoters heard projections.

12. See endnote 17 in Chapter 1.

13. Studies by the Committee for the Study of the American Electorate (1999) found that, prior to the 1993 National Voter Registration Act (NVRA or "Motor Voter"), registration figures in most states were inflated roughly 10 percent with "the names of substantial numbers of citizens who have died or moved." However, NVRA prohibited many common practices used to update the lists, leaving them more cluttered.

14. The extensive study of Portland area voting found a nearly 90 percent turnout rate among of those who were registered and living in their precinct on election day (see Chapter 4). Fuchs, Mendelsohn, the Langs, and others sometimes found even higher rates. The U.S. Census Bureau's November Current Population Surveys have also consistently reported very high turnout rates among registered voters: 86 percent in 2000, 90 percent in 1992, 88 percent in 1984, and 89 percent in 1976.

15. Analyzing the California Poll of January 1981, Percy Tannenbaum and Leslie Kostrich (1983) suspected that faded memories, during two months

when projections were widely denounced in California media, probably increased the proportion of nonvoters who blamed projection beyond that found in more prompt surveys.

16. John E. Jackson merged data from three distinct efforts centered at the University of Michigan's Institute for Social Research—the regular 1980 National Election Study (a large yearlong panel with pre- and postelection surveys), a "Voter Validation Study" conducted by Michigan's Center for Political Studies to check official records to verify respondent voting, and a short telephone reinterview with 1,814 respondents in January 1981. The resulting dataset is available for scholars to study through the Interuniversity Consortium for Political and Social Research.

17. Tannenbaum and Kostrich (1983, p. 66) feared that Jackson's figures translated into a credibility-straining claim that turnout nationwide was reduced 6–11 percent. Epstein and Strom (1984, p. 49) did read Jackson as indicating a 6–12 percent drop in turnout. Sudman (1986, p. 334) extrapolated from Jackson's equations to estimate that 3 or 4 percent in the West were dissuaded from voting. Another interpretation can be drawn from Jackson's comments in the *ISR Newsletter* ("Election Night Projections," 1984) that if all "registered western voters" had heard projections then western turnout would have been 12 percent lower than if none of them heard projections. Since studies (including Chapter 4 in this book) often find that about half of all registered voters in the West hear projections before the polls close, 6 percent seems like a fair deduction from Jackson's estimates. To depress total turnout by 6 percent would mean that one-fourth to one-half of all nonvoting among valid registered voters (a very large majority of whom do vote) would be attributable to (enormously powerful) projections.

18. Remarkable as Jackson's enormous, previously unplanned undertaking was, the two-month delay in conducting interviews took its toll in hazy recollections. For example, three out of ten respondents could offer no estimate of when they heard projection news, and critics doubted the reliability of those who did offer times. Tannenbaum and Kostrich (1983, p. 68) were "uneasy about delayed indirect measures subject to contamination." Sudman (1986, p. 334) was skeptical of Jackson's assumption that faulty recall was random. Epstein and Strom (1984, p. 50) noted that "many people said they heard the [projection] news well before they could have."

19. Epstein and Strom (1984, p. 48) underscored something that Jackson himself acknowledged: "The January survey is neither random nor representative." Jackson's team was unable to complete interviews with 31 percent of the respondents in the original representative NES sample, along with other problems such as entirely omitting residents of Rocky Mountain states.

20. Jackson assigned the entire South (including the half of Dixie on central time) to eastern time and put all the Midwest (including its three large eastern time states) into central time.

21. Epstein and Strom (1984, p. 50) called attention to Jackson's statement: "We use poll closings of 8 pm local time for each region." Actually,

fewer than half of all states closed all their polls at that time, with many states closing their polls at 7:00, and others at 6:00, 7:30, 8:30, or 9:00.

22. Jackson used 6:00 P.M. EST when network coverage began and thus the possibility of being "susceptible to influence by the reporting" (1983, p. 620). However, the key predictor tested was not exposure to TV news after 6:00, but awareness of the projections and Jimmy Carter's early concession. NBC projected Reagan's victory at 8:15 P.M. EST; Carter conceded at 9:52, followed immediately by ABC's projection; the CBS projection came at 10:32.

23. This figure was generous because Epstein and Strom counted nonvoters whose registration status was questionable and because the "Carter was already losing" category could have referred to Carter's early concession and was not confined to blaming projections. Those four people (1 percent of these nonvoters) represent 0.2 percent of the 1,621 potential voters Epstein and Strom identified in the database or 0.3 percent of the 1,252 Jackson says could have voted.

24. Wolfinger and Steven Rosenstone's book *Who Votes?* (1980) was a landmark analysis of the Census Bureau's large periodic Current Population Surveys (CPS), which poll more than 90,000 people. Wolfinger and Linquiti (1981) also likewise took advantage of the CPS typically conducted within two weeks after the November elections; its questions include whether respondents voted in the recent election. Time of voting was also asked in 1972 and 1974, but not in 1976, forcing the use of 1974, a nonpresidential election, as the comparison year.

It should be noted that Census Bureau surveys do not escape the problem of "overreported" voting (Traugott and Katosh, 1979). Also, when using CPS data, one has to hope that westerners, southerners, and northerners exaggerate equally about voting (and randomly about time of voting). Unfortunately, the Census Bureau (1990, p. 26) found that overreporting varied by region and state (e.g., 25 percent in Georgia, 7 percent in California), and changed unevenly over time (e.g., increasing 19 percentage points in Florida in the 1980s, but only 2 percentage points in Oregon).

25. The authors explored whether late-day difference in weather might have shifted turnout, but weather, they wrote, "provides no clues." However, other factors might have influenced who turned out to vote and thus when they voted (cf. Chapter 7). Also, in 1974 (but not in 1972), all five Pacific states elected U.S. senators while many comparison states had no Senate contests.

3

Election Night
Newscasts

Before trying to study the impact of a message, one ought first to assess the message itself. In this case, before studying the impact of projections on voter turnout, it makes sense to examine the nature, frequency, and timing of these projection messages. What did broadcast journalists say and when did they say it?

The times of projection broadcasts have been shown in Table 1.1. As explained in Chapter 1, projections were possible so often and so early due to networks' using exit-poll data (starting in 1980) and their "most polls closed" shortcut (a practice ended in 2002) to take advantage of electoral votes concentrated in the eastern and central time zones, where most polls closed by 8:00 P.M. EST.

In this chapter, special attention is paid, using both qualitative and quantitative content analysis, to broadcasts on election "night" (which begin in the afternoon on the West Coast) in 1984 and 1988 because those years offer particularly good opportunities for studying the impact of projections on voter turnout. First, however, the review turns to the old days when computers were in their infancy.

1960: Computers Unleashed

Researchers have sometimes assumed that the 1960 election must not have involved projections because it was so very close. Remarkably, it did. Proudly featuring their huge primitive mainframe computers being fed early returns, the networks reported probabilities as calculated by the amazing new science fiction–like machines.

At 4:00 P.M. PST, ABC said that the odds from its Univac so far favored Vice President Richard Nixon over Senator John Kennedy by 10 to 1. CBS soon said that its IBM 7090, using "completely inadequate information," had extrapolated that Nixon might amass a Republican landslide of 459 electoral votes. Then, after 5:00 when the first big wave of early returns began to roll in, the ancient computers began to shift over to Democrats. ABC's Univac figured the odds as 7 to 5 favoring Kennedy and CBS's IBM calculated 11 to 5. NBC did not reveal any probabilities until 5:23, when its trusty RCA 501 computer made Kennedy 6.3 to 1 favorite.[1]

The networks were bold to predict, even tentatively, such a tight race—49.7 percent Kennedy versus 49.6 percent Nixon in the final popular vote, with several pivotal states decided by a hair, and disputed returns in Chicago and South Texas. Yet audaciously, CBS estimated Kennedy as probably over the top at 5:14, NBC at 6:03, and ABC at 7:33.[2] While these outputs were treated as novelties needing confirmation by the actual vote count, they contributed to a growing on-air presumption that Kennedy had the clear advantage. In the next election, the tone became more assertive and less qualified.

1964: Preprojection Projections

Lyndon Johnson's landslide victory over Republican Barry Goldwater was treated as a fait accompli almost as soon as coverage began. At 3:48 P.M. PST, while California's sun was still far from the horizon, NBC proclaimed Johnson the "probable" winner and likely to gain 60–70 percent of the popular vote. (LBJ's final count was just over 61 percent, the century's record.) The other networks were also not shy about characterizing the election as trending toward a landslide with Johnson "indicated" as the likely winner, but they did not voice firm projections until after 6:00 P.M. (This election also saw the debut of the Network Election Service, the first joint vote-counting venture by the networks and wire services.)

1968, 1972, 1976: Cliffhangers and a Landslide

In 1968, it was not until the next morning, after enough votes had been counted in the pivotal states of Illinois, Missouri, and California, that

Republican Richard Nixon could be declared the winner. No attempt was made to characterize this election as anything other than extremely close, unexpectedly so in light of Nixon's lead in preelection polls.[3]

Bearing little resemblance to 1968, the 1972 finale saw Nixon sweep forty-nine states and garner almost 61 percent of the popular vote. The networks explicitly projected Nixon's victory quite early—NBC at 5:30 P.M. PST, CBS at 5:50, ABC at 6:20—but for reasons that are not clear, 1972 projections did not provoke the brouhaha that accompanied either the prior projected election in 1964 or the next projected election in 1980. (On election night coverage in 1972, see Pepper, 1973–1974.)

In 1976, Jimmy Carter, the Democrat, and Gerald Ford, the Republican, staged a duel that was unpredictable for most of the night. Carter was not crowned by the networks until after midnight Pacific time. (The reversal of just 9,500 votes in Ohio and Hawaii would have put Ford back in the White House.)

1980: Carter Concedes and NBC Rules

Viewers in 1980 witnessed a bizarre event. For the first time since Alton Parker conceded to Teddy Roosevelt in 1904,[4] a major-party candidate admitted defeat while people on the West Coast were still going to the polls to vote. Jimmy Carter went before the cameras and publicly conceded his loss at 6:52 P.M. PST.

Years earlier, Kurt Lang and Gladys Lang (1968, p. 166) had noted, "Theoretically, a candidate could concede even while balloting was still in progress." "Clearly," they wrote, that is "not likely to occur in fact." But the Langs had not yet met Jimmy Carter, who reportedly had to be persuaded not to concede even earlier. When Carter walked before the cameras, two of the networks had not yet predicted his loss. Many western Democrats were furious that Carter threw in the towel over an hour before their polls closed, at a point when they feared Reagan's Republican surge might overwhelm Democrats in close congressional, state, and local races.[5] Ten-term veteran representative James Corman (D–Calif.) publicly blamed Carter's concession for his narrow defeat.[6]

Others directed their anger at the networks rather than at Carter. It was the projections, they insisted, that had discouraged voting. Stories were told of long lines of people waiting to vote who went home when they heard the news, but these tales were difficult to verify.

If potential voters were discouraged, was it due to Carter quitting or TV projections or both? Some people might have heard NBC's early projection first. Others might have heard about the concession first (which came just before ABC's projection and long before the CBS projection). And many people may have heard about both developments at the same time. Thus, researchers who detected a measurable decline in western voter turnout in 1980 were unable to disentangle whether that decline was due to Carter's concession alone, to the network projections alone, or to some combination of both factors.[7] Despite this analytical quagmire, 1980 prompted the most academic studies of projections and led to contentious congressional hearings.

On that same day something happened on the East Coast that also had profound consequences for projections: NBC ran away with the election. At 5:15 P.M. PST, NBC announced Ronald Reagan's victory. At that point, CBS had only called four states. Another hour would pass before CBS could declare Reagan the winner, long after Jimmy Carter himself had conceded. ABC, while not as slow as CBS, did not come close to matching NBC's blistering pace. As Paul Wilson wrote: "The news of who was winning, it frequently appeared, was somehow the sole province of NBC" (1983, p. 148).

How did NBC do it? The network did not wait for early precinct returns as had been the practice in the past; instead NBC often used exit polls alone. While CBS and ABC patiently assembled actual vote totals, NBC was ready the instant most polls closed in a state.[8] So, for example, when voting ended in Connecticut at 5:00 P.M. PST, NBC called the state for Reagan at 5:01, based on exit polls. Relying on official counts of real votes, ABC was unable to call Connecticut for another hour. NBC had ushered in the brave new world of rapid, exit-poll-based election projections: "Until 1980, all three networks had possessed the nuclear bombs of election projections [exit polls], but had chosen never to use them. When NBC broke this unwritten treaty, the others were then forced to retaliate" (Wilson, 1983, p. 151).

ABC and CBS moved rapidly to incorporate exit polls into their systems for making predictions. The following year they were far more aggressive in covering the gubernatorial race in New Jersey:

> In 1981, both CBS and ABC threw aside tradition, threw aside their earlier Congressional testimony, and threw aside caution. ABC attempted to call a trend in the New Jersey Governor's race two hours before the polls closed and CBS—relying exclusively on exit polling

results—called the race the moment the polls closed. Both ABC and CBS were incorrect in their projections. (Wilson, 1983, pp. 151–152)

Duly chastised by their embarrassing calls in New Jersey, the networks nonetheless redoubled their efforts to exploit exit polls more effectively in the future. ABC and CBS seemed determined not be humiliated again by NBC. And indeed, on election night in 1984 and again in 1988, NBC came in third.

1984: Reagan Announcement Earliest Ever

Thanks to the speed gained by using exit polls and Reagan's forty-nine-state triumph, 1984's projections were, as a group, the earliest ever broadcast. By 5:30 P.M. PST, ABC, CBS, and NBC had all declared Reagan the winner. Unlike the previous Democrat who lost, Walter Mondale reverted to tradition and waited until after West Coast polls closed to concede defeat at 8:20 P.M. PST.

Because the networks all issued unequivocal projections so early *and* no candidate conceded early, the 1984 election is arguably the twentieth century's best single test of whether projections depress voter turnout. Thus, coverage of this election is worth exploring in more detail using data from a qualitative and quantitative content analysis of both television and radio messages during the late afternoon and early evening on the West Coast.[9]

CBS was first. Based on exit polls, seconds after 5:00 P.M. PST — three hours before the polls were to close in the West—Dan Rather intoned: "CBS News estimates that Ronald Reagan has been re-elected President. The questions remains: How big a mandate is he likely to get?" ABC issued its announcement not long after CBS. With far less fanfare than Dan Rather, David Brinkley nonchalantly remarked at 5:13: "We now project the winner in Michigan to be Mr. Reagan, which gives him the electoral votes to make him President for a second term. It gives him a total of 274." Soon, on NBC at 5:30, Tom Brokaw stated: "NBC News is now able to project the re-election of Ronald Wilson Reagan, the 73-year-old President of the United States."

Then throughout the evening, "for those of you just tuning in," the anchormen continually restated their verdict of Reagan's reelection.[10] These reiterations occurred an average of once every twelve minutes between 5:00 and 8:00 (see Table 3.1).

Table 3.1   Election Projections and Exhortations in the 1984 Portland News Media (PST)

	Projections of Reagan's Victory			Exhortations to "Go Vote"		
	5:00–5:59	6:00–6:59	7:00–7:59	5:00–5:59	6:00–6:59	7:00–7:59
TV						
ABC (KATU)	5	6	6	3	3	2
CBS (KOIN)	3	7	4	3	2	—
NBC (KGW)	4	6	5	3	3	2
IND (KPTV)	—	—	1	—	2	1
Radio						
KXL-AM/FM	—	—	—	—	—	—
KYTE-AM	2	2	—	3	—	2
KINK-FM	—	—	—	1	—	—
KGW-AM	—	—	—	—	—	1
KWJJ-AM	1	—	1	1	—	—
KMJK-FM	2	1	—	1	1	—
KGON-FM	—	—	—	1	—	—
KKEY-AM	—	—	—	2	—	—

The word "projection" refers to something estimated, predicted, and necessarily tentative. While anchors did include the word "projects" or "estimates" in first announcements quoted above, from that point forward the verdict was treated as a fact beyond dispute. In Dan Rather's unambiguous words: "Walter Mondale has seen the light at the end of the tunnel—and it's out."

Large maps had only Mondale's Wisconsin painted a different color,[11] and anyone who failed to discern the meaning was told repeatedly: the presidential race was over. Nothing was tentative about it, other than the sheer magnitude of Reagan's victory. Westerners (and many others)[12] were told that the presidential contest had ended before their ballots were counted and before many of them were cast.

Go Vote Anyway

Along with repeated assertions of Reagan's victory, anchormen offered encouragement to those who had not yet voted. Two or three times per hour on each network between 5:00 and 8:00 P.M. PST, westerners were urged to "go vote." Could these injunctions have served as an antidote to the early calls? Perhaps—but closer inspection of the "go vote" comments shows mixed messages.

Often the TV plea to "go vote" reinforced the worthlessness of a late presidential vote. Westerners were urged to vote—even though the presidency was decided—because there were "still" local races to be decided. Here are two of Peter Jennings's exhortations to ABC viewers: "On the West Coast you still have ample time to vote out there. . . . There are still a lot of local races, and there are still some propositions." And, "We're going to remind you again that even though we've projected that the President has enough electoral votes to be re-elected, there are very important races all around the country."

On CBS, the "still go vote" argument had an additional angle. Both Dan Rather and Bill Moyers explained that it was not too late for westerners to at least help determine whether Ronald Reagan would have a "blank check" or be "balanced" by Democrats in Congress, even if westerners would have no voice in Reagan's reelection.

Over at NBC, Tom Brokaw was also telling viewers that they "still" ought to go vote anyway: "We do want to remind you, however, that there are still important issues to be settled and important races to be settled as well."

Conceivably, such appeals might have spurred people to vote—but it is also possible that they inadvertently trivialized late votes by embedding yet another reminder that the most important contest in the country was over.[13]

Characterizations

The term "characterizations" has been used to describe another controversial aspect in election coverage. Hours before the first formal projections, TV reporters sometimes "characterized" the progress of the voting based on exit surveys. In doing so, they implied who was winning at the polls but stopped short of declaring the winner. A few listeners might not catch the qualification ("if current trends continue") and may interpret characterization hints as tantamount to a projection.

ABC won plaudits from elected officials for announcing a ban on early preprojection characterizations in 1984. In practice, ABC did air a few general characterizations.[14] CBS and NBC, on the other hand, made no pretense of abandoning their reporting of early trends. For example, Rather began the CBS coverage by saying that "a substantial win for Ronald Reagan may—may—be borne out if the voting trends don't change."

On NBC, early tentative portrayals of trends soon became increasingly less tentative: "what looks like a landslide victory" (Wallace), "a commanding lead" (Brokaw). Such strong characterizations of voting trends began in the middle of the afternoon (3:30 P.M. PST on CBS), a full four and a half hours before West Coast polls closed.

In the years that followed, the networks sometimes promised not to "characterize" election trends. Nevertheless, in their hints and assumptions, anchors and commentators have not always entirely concealed that information.

Radio

A neglected aspect of the media environment on election day is radio. As people drive home from work, hearing radio's ricochet of TV projections might possibly influence their decision of whether to stop at the polls. Until now, there has been no systematic study of whether radio stations in the West tend to amplify or ignore TV projections. To begin to address this question, research conducted for this book used Portland, Oregon, as the site for a content analysis of radio coverage. (Reasons for focusing on the Portland area are reviewed early in Chapter 4.) The goal was to measure the extent to which radio news and disc jockey banter relayed and reinforced network projections.

If radio did relay the news often, projections would be heard by an enormous audience. Arbitron surveys in the fall of 1984 showed that 77 percent of all Portland metro-area voting-age adults listened to the radio at least five minutes during the 3:00–7:00 P.M. period. Roughly half of the listeners (64 percent of the men and 42 percent of the women) were at work or in the car or otherwise "away from home" during this "P.M. drive time." In the Portland area (as in most of the West throughout the 1960–2000 period), over 80 percent of the work force commuted to their jobs in private automobiles, according to the Census Bureau.

As many people rode or prepared to ride home and perhaps considered stopping to vote, what messages did they hear on the radio? To track radio content, eight Portland radio stations, four AM and four FM, were selected for study on the basis of their large audience share and wide variety of formats. These stations included top 40, big band, adult pop, country and western, easy listening, album-oriented rock, and talk radio. Arbitron rated these eight stations as reaching about half of all late-afternoon adult radio listeners (see Table 3.2). A total of twenty-four hours of Portland radio content was analyzed, three hours (5:00–8:00 P.M.) for each of the eight stations.

Content findings were surprising. Five of the eight radio stations had a total blackout of early projection news. Before Oregon polls closed, Reagan's network-proclaimed victory was not mentioned once on these five stations. Their newscasters ignored it and disc jockeys did not chatter about it (see Table 3.1).

The three other radio stations did not exactly bombard their audiences with the news. Listeners of KYTE-AM would have learned about Reagan's victory if they happened to hear one of the five-minute "news on the hour" segments. At 5:00, KYTE aired Charles Osgood on CBS Radio News, who began with this lead story: "We now show President Reagan over the 270 mark in terms of electoral votes based on our exit polling. . . . President Reagan has won." This comment was an exception, however. Unless radio listeners happened to catch certain stations at certain times, they heard lots of music and no projections. From 5:00 until 8:00, on the three stations that did mention the subject, a total of only seven projections were aired during newscasts, and only twice did disc jockeys mention it.

For this three-hour period, four additional variables were counted: (1) paid campaign commercials, (2) injunctions to listeners to "go vote," (3) promotions of a station's own forthcoming election-return news, and (4) explicit discussions of the merits of early projections. Paid campaign commercials were rarely aired late on election day, typically only one or two spots. Nor did radio stations push their listeners

Table 3.2   Leading Portland Radio Stations

	Share (%)	1984 Radio Format
KXL-AM/FM	11.1	Contemporary easy listening
KYTE-AM	7.3	Big band and vocals
KINK-FM	6.5	Album-oriented rock
KGW-AM	6.4	Adult pop
KWJJ-AM	5.4	Country and western
KMJK-FM	4.1	Top 40
KGON-FM	3.6	Album-oriented rock
KKEY-AM	2.2	All talk and sports

Source: Adult audience share in "P.M. drive time" (3:00–7:00) Arbitron ratings, Portland, Fall 1984.

to go vote. The typical station offered one "go vote" appeal during this period.

Three of the five stations that blacked out network projections did air promotions of their own forthcoming coverage, conspicuously timed to begin after local polls closed. On KGW, for example: "Be sure and be listening to us tonight beginning exactly at 8:01 when the polls close; our news team is going to run down the results. . . . All that coverage beginning here at 8:01 exactly this evening." The projection controversy was only mentioned once, by KYTE's Dave Collins, who denounced the practice in no uncertain terms. In his extended tirade, he called projections "unfair, immoral, and certainly unconstitutional."

Overall, radio listeners heard little about the election and very rarely heard projection news. The restraint exercised by these stations must have seriously limited the diffusion of projection news, reducing the chances that those who had not yet voted might hear network verdicts via radio.

1988: Bush Wins Early

In 1988, by 6:21 P.M. PST, both ABC and CBS had named Republican George H. W. Bush as the winner over Democrat Michael Dukakis; NBC did not project Bush until 7:30. Dukakis waited until 8:15 to concede after West Coast polls closed. Earlier in the evening on CBS, Dan Rather had said that "buzzards are starting to circle over Dukakis' chances." Then, at 6:17, Rather declared: "Our CBS news estimate is that George Bush will be the next President of the United States and that Dan Quayle will be the next Vice President of the United States. . . . It's over. George Bush wins. Carries Quayle in with him." CBS frequently repeated its projection another nineteen times before 7:00 and twenty-two times from 7:00 to 8:00. Soon after CBS's projection, Peter Jennings of ABC announced: "Based on projections in the states where the polls have closed, George Bush has the electoral votes required to be the next president."

Despite this early announcement at 6:21, ABC rarely repeated it during the next hour. Was ABC trying to appease critics by spending less time emphasizing Bush's projected victory? At 7:30, Jennings was almost apologetic about the early projection and about not mentioning it much: "It may be . . . that we're tiptoeing around the story of the night here. Even though the polls have not closed in the West. . . . It's just so easy to put together the 270 electoral votes while not hearing from Oregon and Washington and California and Hawaii and Alaska." From that point on, with only a half hour left before West Coast polls closed, ABC frequently reiterated its projection of Bush (see Table 3.3).

At 7:30, NBC's Tom Brokaw broke the news sardonically: "George Bush, who has been living in government housing for the past eight years, will continue to live in government housing. He'll move from Massachusetts Avenue to 1600 Pennsylvania Avenue. NBC News now projects that George Bush is president-elect of the United States." NBC repeated the projection ten times during the 7:30–8:00 period. (For 1988 projection methods, see Mitofsky, 1991.)

As usual, "go vote" messages sent mixed signals as Tom Brokaw made sure that westerners were not under any illusion that their votes would matter in electing the president:

> In the far West and the Pacific Northwest, polls do remain open. They'll be open for another twenty minutes or so. There are some important races still to be resolved out there. You'll want to cast your vote for the presidential candidate of your choice—and you still have the opportunity to do so—but the fact of the matter is the Vice-President of the United States was able to win enough electoral votes in those states that you see [on the map] behind me to go over the top, past the 270 figure.

1992: The Latest Early Projections

The 1992 projections were broadcast before West Coast polls closed, but just barely. Despite earlier intimations of a forthcoming Democratic victory,[15] not until 7:48 P.M. PST did all three networks project Bill

Table 3.3   1988 Election Projections and Exhortations (PST)

	Projections of Bush's Victory		Exhortations to "Go Vote"	
	6:00–6:59	7:00–7:59	6:00–6:59	7:00–7:59
ABC	2	15	3	3
CBS	20	22	3	2
NBC	—	10	3	3

Clinton as the winner over George Bush and Ross Perot.[16] Only a dozen minutes were left before polls closed on the West Coast. Perot, an unusually strong third-party candidate, had conceded early (7:32), but Bush, the Republican incumbent, waited until shortly after 8:00.

The simultaneous projections at 7:48 were due to the networks' pooling of their exit-poll operations in order to cut costs. Not only was the data collection shared, but data analysis was conducted jointly as well. The reason for the delay in projections was due to close contests in several big states such as Texas, Florida, and Ohio. Once they were sufficiently resolved, Rather was emphatic both about Clinton's election and about CBS's not yet blemished record: "According to our CBS News estimate, that's it. Game, set, match. It's over. We will have a new President of the United States. CBS News has never been wrong in making these calls in a Presidential race—underscore the word 'never.' . . . Bill Clinton will be the new President of the United States."

1996: Dole Concedes Early

As in 1992, the 1996 projections were announced virtually in unison.[17] At 6:00 P.M. PST, President Bill Clinton was declared reelected. Clinton's margin of victory was not nearly as large as most preelection polls had predicted, but the Republican challenger Senator Bob Dole still did not come close to an upset.

Shortly after the projections, anchors read a concession statement just issued by Dole's press secretary. Dole thus earned the dubious distinction of quitting almost two hours before West Coast polls closed, even earlier than Jimmy Carter had conceded in 1980. Realizing their error, Dole's camp tried to undo the damage by attempting to retract the concession forty-five minutes later. Then, at 8:25, Dole's swan song was reissued. Once again, as with Carter's early concession in 1980, any dampening effects due to early projections would be entwined with Dole's initial, astonishingly early concession.

2000: Projection Debacles

Ironically, the most controversial single night (and early morning) for election projections came in November 2000, when the networks did *not* project the nationwide winner before West Coast polls closed. Instead, among other things, the networks rapidly awarded the pivotal state of Florida to Democrat Al Gore based on faulty data and erroneously announced that all polls in Florida were closed when polls were still open in western Florida. Then they retracted the Florida call for Gore and a few hours later projected Florida for Republican George W. Bush, anointing him the next president. Then, having prompted a concession from Al Gore, they retracted their verdict for Bush and concluded that Florida was still too close to call. These extraordinary projection errors and related controversies are reviewed in more detail in Chapter 9.

During the 2000 election, ABC, CBS, and NBC were still the undisputed ratings champions. They no longer had a near monopoly as in previous decades, but they still were the dominant troika. During prime time of election night 2000, NBC alone earned higher ratings than the combined total of CNN, Fox News, MSNBC, and PBS. To be sure, cable news competitors were making gains, but in 2000, ABC, CBS, and NBC still dominated U.S. television news.

2004: Internet Leaks by Day and Caution by Night

Neither Senator John Kerry nor President George W. Bush was ever projected as the winner at any time by any networks. Yet once again the spotlight of controversy focused on exit polls and projections with a new twist in 2004.

Throughout election day, preliminary exit poll results were, thanks to the Internet, far more widely disseminated than ever before. Unweighted results leaked from morning exit polls—tilting markedly to John Kerry—ricocheted rapidly around Slate.com, DrudgeReport.com, and a multitude of Internet blogs. During the afternoon, websites buzzed with claims of a pending Kerry victory, Reuters spread the leaks further via its wire service, on Wall Street the Dow Jones index fell, a few television commentators began to suggest that Bush was in trouble, and major newspapers drafted stories based on that presumption. While music radio stations may have largely ignored the rumors,[18] some talk radio commentators like Sean Hannity and Rush Limbaugh did note the leaks and disputed their accuracy but urged their listeners to redouble their efforts nonetheless. Although no actual network projections were broadcast, some analysts speculated that the rumors and leaks must have energized Kerry's followers to vote and to work harder for the

Democrats, while discouraging Bush supporters from voting and from volunteering for "get-out-the-vote" efforts.

The initial numbers were often so extremely one-sided—such as showing Kerry with a 20 percentage point lead in Pennsylvania, a state he ultimately won by only 2 percentage points—that they should have been greeted with far more skepticism. Yet, nearing the climax of a bitterly fought campaign, many partisans, bloggers, talk radio hosts, and mainstream journalists gave the early exit polls more weight than they deserved. As afternoon data were added, estimates of Kerry's standing shrank but continued to be inflated.

By the end of the day, the National Election Pool's exit polls were found to have exaggerated Kerry's vote by about 2 percentage points. One of the directors, Warren Mitofsky, attributed this gap to a slightly higher refusal rate among Republicans than among Democrats. Because some Republicans increasingly view the traditional news media as close allies of the Democrats, they may have been a bit more likely to reject the survey page that prominently featured TV network logos at the top.

In any event, actual votes soon showed Bush clearly surpassing his 2000 totals in state after state (even increasing his share of the vote in Kerry's home base of Massachusetts by 5 percentage points) and confirmed that the final exit-poll numbers slightly underestimated Bush's votes. Network decisionmakers, already inclined to be careful as penance for their errors in the 2000 election, quickly became even more cautious. Rather than rely too much on exit-poll estimates, the networks often turned more to actual vote counts as compiled by the Associated Press. As a result, none of the networks made erroneous projections of any state.

With so much caution, the usual race to be first came to a screeching halt in 2004. The new pressure was to avoid a premature call that might backfire.[19]

ABC was the first to call Florida for Bush, but not until long after the polls had closed in both Florida time zones. ABC's call came at 8:40 P.M. PST (11:40 EST), with CBS calling it five minutes later. With Bush having a seemingly solid hold on Florida and Kerry on Pennsylvania, Ohio soon emerged as the pivotal swing state, where Bush had a large lead but "provisional ballots" added a wildcard. At 9:40 P.M. PST Fox called Ohio for Bush, with NBC soon following suit.

At that point, viewers witnessed one of the oddest projection dances ever seen on election night. The networks adamantly refused to call the election for Bush. Neither NBC nor Fox would award Nevada for Bush, a move that would have given Bush a majority of the electoral vote. Conversely, ABC, CBS, and CNN gave Nevada to Bush but resisted calling Ohio. CNN's Jeff Greenfield admitted, "If we hadn't gone through what we'd gone through in 2000, we probably would have called Ohio for Bush."[20] On the *Today Show,* Tom Brokaw said that NBC was intentionally holding back too: "Our judgment is that we will not be the arbiter. There will be no declaration from us tonight as long as the Kerry campaign is contesting in Ohio."

Indeed, Kerry representatives were pleading with the networks not to declare Bush the winner, just as the Bush campaign was urging the networks to put their seal on a Bush victory. But no network wanted to risk another colossal mistake on the scale of their blunders in 2000. Better to wait and see what John Kerry was going to do than to tell him what to do. At the conclusion of a tense and bitter campaign, Kerry's team was able to assess the situation in Ohio independently, without the added albatross of already having been declared the loser by the nation's networks. Later Wednesday morning, Senator Kerry called the White House to concede the election to President Bush.

Despite the brouhaha about the leaked exit polls during the day, the networks avoided projection errors on election night. They were exceedingly cautious about calling individual states and never crowned Bush the winner. In contrast to early projections, the slower pacing did not prompt viewer anger. TV stations were not besieged by irate viewers complaining that the networks had projected too slowly and too timidly. To try to deal with the problem of leaked exit polls, it was later announced that in the future, exit-poll data would not begin to be distributed to clients until late afternoon.

In many ways, 2004 represents the passing of an era in broadcast news not just because of the unprecedented caution in issuing projections or because of the postelection retirement of two men who had been lead anchors for decades—Dan Rather of CBS and Tom Brokaw of NBC. Challenges to the dominance of the heretofore almost invincible "big three" were vividly symbolized by two developments. One of them, illustrating the new power of alternative media, was when a featured exposé that CBS's *60 Minutes* had been investigating for four years was discredited within twenty-four hours by Internet bloggers.

The other evidence of a reconfigured media world was that upstart Fox News jumped into the top tier on election night. While NBC, with 15.2 million viewers, was again the most watched network for prime-time election night coverage, Fox attracted an astonishing 12.8 million viewers to its cable news (8.1 million viewers) and its news on its broadcast stations (4.7 million viewers). According to Nielsen ratings, the Fox total surpassed CBS's 9.5 million viewers and rivaled ABC's 13.2 million. Fifth-place CNN had 6.2 million viewers.

Newscast Messages

Certainly, presidential projections are not the only interesting communication from TV newscasts on the afternoon and evening of election day. Throughout the shows, anchors and correspondents weave an ongoing narrative, usually with a few subplots.[21] Their storyline serves to frame their interpretations of unfolding events and ties things together.

Instant analysis of exit-poll data then lets reporters quickly propose the reasons for victories and defeats around the nation.[22] One theme may center on a subgroup designated as the trendy one to watch ("soccer Moms," "NASCAR Dads," "Reagan Democrats"). The status of key Senate and House races will be monitored, with extra attention to the more intriguing sagas. Yet, at least until 2004, all else has paled beside the quest to call enough states to assemble the 270 electoral votes needed to project the winning presidential candidate. Having put polls, strategies, and the question of who is winning the presidential horse race at the center of coverage for much of the year (Farnsworth and Lichter, 2003; Patterson, 2002, 1993, 1980; Patterson and McClure, 1976; Robinson and Sheehan, 1983), the networks traditionally had sustained that priority on election day using exit polls and projections to try to advance the horse-race results by a few hours.

From the moment those projections were broadcast, they were then treated as unassailable statements of fact. News anchors frequently repeated the verdict "for those just tuning in." Even when westerners were urged to "still go vote" for "local races," they were often reminded that they were not relevant to the presidential race. Broadcasting projections in this manner has important implications for their dissemination and impact. Their frequent repetition means that anyone turning on a TV set would rarely have wait long to be told that the race for the White House was absolutely over. With this sort of news media output, what proportion of potential voters in the West hear about projections before the polls close? And how many of the people who hear that news are decisively pushed not to cast a ballot? These two questions become the focus in Chapter 4.

Notes

1. "Special Report," *Broadcasting,* November 14, 1960, p. 42. Watching NBC's Chet Huntley and David Brinkley forty years later, Jean Folkert (2000) was struck by how the tone was so "serious, calm, understated, and patient" as election returns unfolded in 1960, unlike the frenetic pace of later years.

2. "Special Report," *Broadcasting,* November 14, 1960, p. 42.

3. Sam Tuchman and Thomas Coffin (1971) conducted a large survey of nearly 2,000 voters immediately before and after the projection-free 1968 election. TV's election night message that the race was "too close to call" did *not* stimulate turnout, they concluded. Their study would have been about projections if Richard Nixon's late-October lead had held, but by election day it was a close contest that was not decided until the next morning.

4. At 5:25 P.M. PST (*New York Times,* November 9, 1904).

5. K. Reich, "State Democrats Bitter on Carter's Early Concession," *Los Angeles Times,* November 5, 1980, p. 3; R. Smith, "Early Concession Crippled Vote Effort," *Los Angeles Times,* November 7, 1980, p. 1.

6. "Corman Blames Early Carter Concession," *Los Angeles Times,* November 5, 1980, p. 1.

7. See Jackson, 1983; and Dubois, 1983.

8. For a thorough analysis of how news organizations designed and administered exit surveys in 1980 using "thousands of journalists, analysts, interviewers, computer programmers, data clerks, and others," see Levy, 1983. On network polling in general during this period, see Sudman, 1983. For a useful critique of reporters' techniques of instant interpretations of voter behavior, see Joslyn, Ross, and Weinstein, 1984.

9. Quantitative content analysis is designed to count, as objectively and consistently as possible, how often the material under study (e.g., books, articles, broadcasts, letters, speeches) includes specific messages (perhaps particular words, phrases, assertions, issues, themes, sources, or visual images). Basic steps are to (1) decide the study's scope and collect the material to be analyzed, (2) define a clear, explicit way to measure and code each variable, (3) verify and refine the reliability of the measurement system by testing if different coders usually reach identical conclusions when coding the same material, (4) code all material under study, and (5) tally and analyze the findings (see Adams and Schreibman, 1978; Krippendorf, 1981; Weber, 1990; and Neuendorf, 2001). Increasingly sophisticated computer software can also be employed to count and detect patterns (West, 2001).

Content data in this chapter analyzed 5:00–8:00 P.M. PST election-day coverage by the three networks in 1984 and 1988, and by the eight major Portland radio stations in 1984. (A sample was not used, so inferential statistics are not necessary.) The variables coded were uncomplicated ones, such as "projections," defined as an unambiguous, unequivocal statement that a candidate had won the presidency. None of the intercoder reliability scores for the reported variables were lower than 0.98, meaning that when different coders (three in this case) reviewed the same material, their coding was at least 98 percent identical for each variable.

More subjective variables yield much lower intercoder reliability scores. For example, "characterizations" (suggestions of voting trends that stop short of an explicit projection) can range from gentle hints to major trend statements. Characterizations were not successfully coded with a high degree of reliability, so verbatim examples are presented to illustrate their tone and make the general point that they were voiced prior to the more formal "projections."

For widely varied examples of content analyses of TV news, see Adams, 2003, 1987, 1985a, 1985b, 1984, 1983, 1982, 1981, 1978; and Adams and Albin, 1980.

10. As usual, many westerners were infuriated by the projections. Portland's *Oregonian* reported (November 7, 1984) that TV stations were "deluged with protest calls," producing "swamped" switchboards from thousands of people who were "really livid." On Portland's ABC affiliate (KATU-TV) responding to angry viewers, a young Bill O'Reilly in one of his first jobs as a local TV anchorman (twenty years before hosting the highest rated show in cable news) contended that ABC was using more restraint than were its competitors (5:58 P.M. PST, November 6, 1984): "Exit-polling projections or predictions are made while the state polls are still open. Now we are not doing that here at Channel Two, and ABC is not doing that, but the other two networks are." In fact, ABC was not waiting until all polls closed in dual-zone states before projecting those states.

11. At the time, colors were not consistent across networks. Not until the 1990s did all three networks assign Republicans red and Democrats blue, oddly reversing the colors that since the French Revolution in 1789 have been associated worldwide with the Left and the Right.

12. Regarding people living as far east as Rhode Island sometimes being exposed to projections before their state's polls close, see the discussion for Figures 1.3 and 1.4.

13. In focus groups (Chapter 8), some westerners seemed to consider such injunctions to be condescending. A woman from California said, "I don't like it when Jennings and Rather tell us we ought to go vote for dog-catcher 'cause they and their friends already elected the president."

14. For example, about an hour before ABC's formal projections, ABC's Steve Bell commented that "one of the big questions tonight" is the strength of "Ronald Reagan's coattails for members of the Senate and House." Presumably, only the winner could have coattails.

15. Dan Rather (5:03 P.M. PST): "We are not prepared to say that there's a winner in the Presidential race not, not yet. But clearly, listen, you can look, you can hear. . . . Bill Clinton has jumped out to a very large early lead." Dan Rather (6:45 P.M. PST): "He [Bill Clinton] can see it, he can smell it, he can taste it, but as of this second does not, not yet have it."

16. Perot's maverick candidacy gained 19 percent of popular vote and was estimated to have boosted voter turnout by 3 percent points nationwide (Lacy

and Burden, 1999). For a thorough account of how 1992 exit polls were conducted, see Mitofsky, 1995.

17. See Merkle and Edelman, 2000, for a detailed review of how the Voter News Service conducted its 1996 exit polls.

18. Echoing the research of Portland radio in 1984, a forthcoming study (Adams and Schmerbeck, 2005) of the 2004 election day output of ten varied California radio stations in the Santa Barbara and San Francisco markets again found that music radio stations took little notice of early returns or network projections of eastern states.

19. Unfortunately, during delays before calling states, the misleading phrase "too close to call" was often used on the air, suggesting that Bush and Kerry were locked in a tight battle in a state. In fact, the inability to call a state promptly after its polls closed was often due to inadequate information rather than the race being particularly close. Using a much better phrase, CBS posted the words "insufficient data" by the names of states that had not yet been called.

20. Quoted in David Bauder, "Television Networks Proceed Cautiously," Associated Press, November 3, 2004.

21. Edward Epstein (1973, pp. 4–5) quoted NBC News producer Reuven Frank instructing: "Every news story should, without any sacrifice of probity or responsibility, display the attributes of fiction, of drama. It should have structure and conflict, problem and denouement, rising action and falling action, a beginning, a middle, and an end." See also Weaver, 1975.

22. Patterson, 2003; Joslyn, Ross, and Weinstein, 1984.

4

Polling Portland's Nonvoters:
Western Oregon

What happened after all three networks hit the West with the earliest un-equivocal projection ever broadcast? The year was 1984 and the verdicts aired within a narrow span of thirty minutes from 5:00 to 5:30 P.M. PST, up to three hours before West Coast polls closed. That night, as part of the research for this book, brief interviews were conducted with 1,258 registered voters in the Portland area of western Oregon. Their answers showed the diffusion of projection news and its reported impact on voter turnout. Before turning to the results, two preliminary matters should be addressed first: Why 1984 and why the Portland area?

Why 1984?

Overall, 1984 appears to have been a very good test, thanks to ex-tremely early projections that were not confounded by an early conces-sion. However, Seymour Sudman viewed 1984 as a poor year for a test because "the substantial victory for Reagan had been anticipated" long before election day (1986, p. 333). He argued that projections could have an independent impact only when they are unexpected, as was said to have been the case in 1980; otherwise, they merely confirm the obvious winner.[1]

While it may have merit, this "shock theory" is not self-evident. One can just as easily argue the opposite: voters may be *less* inclined to trust the reliability of a surprising early projection, while they may be *more* convinced by—and more prepared to act on—the accuracy of an early projection that confirms their suspicions. After all, research repeatedly finds mass communication to be more persuasive and credible when the message reinforces preconceptions.

Another problem with a shock theory of projections is its false premise of retrospectively "obvious landslides." Sudman supposed that everyone knew Ronald Reagan would be a big winner over Walter Mondale. In fact, the preelection National Election Study (NES) found that 48 percent anticipated a close race. Only 46 percent expected the victor (some predicted Mondale) to "win by quite a bit." Americans do not obediently accept the wisdom of the nation's pollsters. As is almost always the case, most people did not take the outcome for granted in 1984.[2]

Are potential voters likely to be influenced more by discordant (unexpected) projections or by confirmatory (expected) projections—or by both or by neither? In 1984, the NES study found, about half of the electorate should have been inclined to find projections to be confirmatory and about half discordant. So, whether or not shock theory has any merit, 1984 still serves as a good full-strength test of projections.

Why Oregon?

During presidential elections, five states—Alaska, Hawaii, Washington, California, and Oregon (minus one county)—plus northern Idaho, have the latest poll closings and receive the longest exposure to projections. In searching for an area to survey intensely, Oregon attracted attention because in the previous election a prominent congressman, Al Ullman, had been narrowly upset in his bid for reelection.

Ullman's supporters blamed his defeat on the TV networks, arguing that early calls of Republican victory discouraged many Democrats from voting. Critics saw his narrow loss as a perfect example of the mischief that might be wrought when TV anchors announce that the presidential election is "over" hours before the polls close in the West.

Since the Ullman district was an alleged "scene of the crime," why not return to that scene for a closer inspection under similar circumstances? Adjoining Ullman's old territory was a similar competitive district, Oregon's First District, represented by Democrat Les AuCoin. In 1984 this district was regarded as one to watch. Republicans were enthusiastic about the chances of Bill Moshofsky, who had almost defeated AuCoin in 1982. Thus this district was a model venue for purposes of this survey—a competitive western congressional race where projections were feared as having the potential to change the outcome, and were believed in some quarters to have done just that to nearby Al Ullman four years earlier.

Survey Design

Lessons developed in Chapter 2 set the goals: a large election night survey starting the instant polls closed (before memories faded) involving telephoning those who were registered but did not vote that day (verified by official records) while trying to minimize false claims of voting. To begin, a random sample of eighty precincts was selected in urban and suburban Portland (Multnomah and Washington Counties) as well as in more rural parts of the district (Yamhill County). The AuCoin campaign graciously provided lists of current telephone numbers for registered voters in these precincts.

With the cooperation of local authorities, precinct records were checked by 8:00 P.M. (usually starting five or ten minutes early) to identify nonvoters, whose names were then circled as targets on the phone lists. Researchers then rushed to seven phone banks set up around the district (including local colleges and the Nike headquarters). Telephoning known nonvoters who were eligible to vote, efforts continued until 10:15–10:30, when people began to complain about being called so late.

Only 16 percent of those contacted refused to be surveyed. This low refusal rate may be due to the excitement of the evening, effective college-educated interviewers, and truthfully stating at the outset that the survey "takes less than two minutes." Also, telemarketing, answering machines, and call screening had not yet begun to do so much damage to response rates.[3]

As noted in Chapter 2, past surveys often suffered losses of large numbers of nonvoters who refused to admit what official records showed—that they had not cast a ballot. The Portland-area survey made a sizable improvement. Whether due to the exculpatory question wording,[4] sympathetic interviewers, forthright Oregonians, or all three, only 9 percent of the known nonvoters claimed to have voted, making it possible to complete successful interviews with many more admitted nonvoters.

Calls from Oregon were supplemented by George Washington University students in Washington, D.C., working from the entire precinct telephone lists and thus surveying mostly voters, but catching nonvoters as well. Thanks to many effective volunteers and coordinators,[5] it was possible to survey 639 nonvoters who were verified as registered and eligible to vote and confirmed by official poll books as not having voted.[6] From the same precincts, 619 voters were also surveyed. The basic confidence intervals for each sample at the usual 95 percent level of probability is ±4 percent.

News Diffusion

On CBS, Ronald Reagan was declared the winner at 5:00 P.M. PST (Tuesday, November 6, 1984), but of course that news was not instantly conveyed to everyone in the West. With three hours remaining before local polls closed, Oregonians had a long time to find out about the projection. But did they? "News junkies" may forget that other Americans do not follow the news as devoutly as they do. Even in the midst of a presidential election, many people go about their daily routines without being enthralled by newscasts. How rapidly were the network projections disseminated? The survey data from Oregon offer some interesting answers.

When?

Respondents were asked if and when they had heard about projections (in a way that would allow for learning about projections indirectly as well as directly): "Did you hear anywhere today that a TV network had declared Reagan as the winner?" And if yes, "As exactly as you can remember, what time was that?"

Diffusion was not nearly as rapid or widespread as one might assume. Six out of ten of nonvoting registered voters (58 percent) did *not* hear projections before the polls closed. Thus, a majority of nonvoters were never "at risk" because TV's potentially discouraging words never reached them, directly or indirectly. Voters were somewhat *more* likely than nonvoters to have heard about the network projections.[7] Just over half of the voters (54 percent) did hear about the projections before 8:00 P.M.

Starting with those who first heard a projection around 5:00, Figure 4.1 shows the dissemination of projection news in quarter-hour intervals. Although somewhat more voters than nonvoters heard the news, the relative diffusion pattern was similar for both groups. Most people who heard about projections got the news during the first two hours. Despite the large unaware audience remaining, diffusion began to plateau by just the third hour.

Who?

Political scientist V. O. Key (1963) suggested that one consequence of a presidential campaign was to accentuate differences in information levels between the more and the less educated. Communications schol-

Figure 4.1 Cumulative Diffusion of Projection News Among Voters and Nonvoters

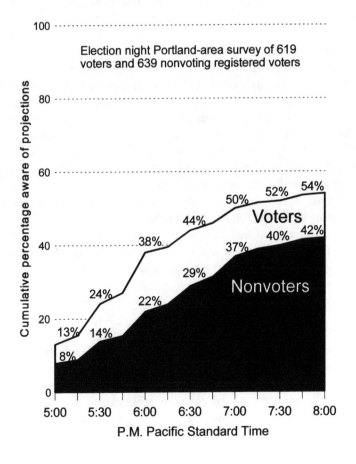

Election night Portland-area survey of 619 voters and 639 nonvoting registered voters

ars call this the "knowledge gap hypothesis": mass media information increases the knowledge gap between groups of higher and lower socioeconomic status because better-educated people acquire information from the news media more often and more easily (Tichenor, Donohue, and Olien, 1970). However, in this case, those who had attended college were not significantly more likely to have heard about projections before 8:00 P.M. than were those who never attended college.

In addition to education, other factors were examined, including age, sex, party identification, urban-suburban-rural residence, and presidential preference. None proved to be a significant predictor of exposure to projections. The sole modest predictors of exposure were both measures of political interest: whether respondents voted and whether they watched a televised debate, a variable that captures political interest mixed with television affinity. Among all respondents, 55 percent of those who had previously watched the Reagan-Mondale debates were aware of projections before 8:00 P.M., compared to 40 percent among those who had not watched the debates.

Having watched a televised debate is not an extremely strong predictor of projection awareness, but it was the strongest one found. The relationship suggests at least some purposive behavior (people who are more politically engaged tend to get more election news), although one might have expected stronger evidence of eagerness to check the breaking news. At the same time, among those who neither voted nor watched a debate, 33 percent had heard projection news—perhaps in ways that tended to be more casual or accidental.

Despite three hours of diffusion time, over half of the nonvoters and almost half of the voters did *not* hear the news before the polls closed, apparently neither in a rush to find out nor exposed inadvertently. This limited dissemination curtails the maximum impact that projections could have if they do influence voter turnout.

How?

Oregonians who had heard about a projection were asked: "Did you hear this on the radio, from another person, or from watching TV yourself?" Watching television firsthand was the most common way—for 42 percent of the voters and 29 percent of the nonvoters (see Figure 4.2). The greater exposure of voters to projection news came entirely from watching television, suggesting more purposive, not accidental, exposure.

Figure 4.2   Sources of Projection News

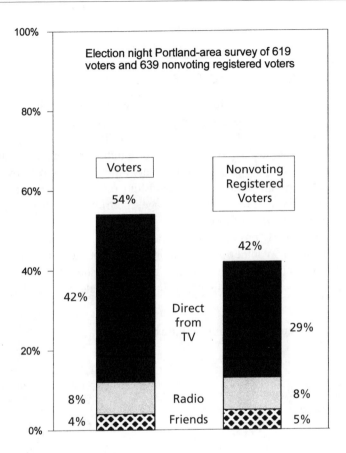

Radio was the conduit for 8 percent of both voters and nonvoters. This may seem a little high in light of Chapter 3's content analysis. Between 5:00 and 8:00 P.M. on eight leading radio stations, five never mentioned projection news, one did so twice, one three times, and one four times. Yet Portland radio reaches 77 percent of all area adults during "P.M. drive time," so it is entirely feasible that 8 percent might have heard one of those mentions.

Only 4–5 percent of those surveyed said they first learned of projection news by hearing about it from another person, perhaps as a passive recipient since voters and nonvoters varied little in this regard.

This modest amount of interpersonal transmission may be due in part to the time of day when fewer people are congregated at work. Projections may also be too mundane to prompt friends to alert one another to the news.

Diffusion of News About Other Events

Projections had low diffusion rates compared to many news events. Table 4.1 summarizes the extent of public awareness of assorted news within ninety minutes after the announcement. Paradoxically, "media stories" that move fastest do so by word of mouth. Breaking news that reached over half of the public within ninety minutes was spread by interpersonal communication to more than four out of ten of those who got the news. Even in the mass media age, the truly rapid diffusion of news depends on word of mouth.

In Oregon, early projections were rarely amplified by interpersonal communications. Whether due to the time of day or lack of interest or both, TV projections did not stimulate the interpersonal buzz required for rapid and widespread dissemination. Nevertheless, among those

Table 4.1   Comparative Diffusion Rates

Diffusion Within 90 Minutes (% aware)	News Event	Source		Research Setting[a]
		Mass Media (%)	Interpersonal (%)	
99	Death of Franklin Roosevelt	11	87	Kent State
95	Assassination of John Kennedy	43	57	Dallas
92	Assassination of John Kennedy	47	49	Nationwide
90	Shooting of Ronald Reagan	55	45	Indianapolis
65	Shooting of Pope John Paul	58	42	Cleveland
61	Shooting of George Wallace	56	44	New York
50	Resignation of Spiro Agnew	28	72	Harvard
45	Launching of Explorer I satellite	77	23	Lansing
39	Eisenhower to seek 2nd term	80	20	Palo Alto
38	1984 TV election projections	92	8	Portland
31	Eisenhower's stroke	82	18	Lansing
7	Alaska statehood approved	98	2	Madison

Note: a. Kent State: Miller (1945); Dallas: Hill and Bonjean (1965); nationwide: Sheatsley and Feldman (1964); Indianapolis: Gantz (1983); Cleveland: Quarles et al. (1983); New York: Schwartz (1973); Harvard: Fine (1975); Lansing: Deutschmann and Danielson (1960); Palo Alto: Danielson (1956), awareness of 39 percent based on slightly more than two hours; Lansing and Madison: Deutschmann and Danielson (1960).

who were exposed, however it happened, projections may have influenced their inclination to vote.

Explanations for Not Voting

A remarkable range of explanations were given for not voting.[8] Before the questionnaire made any mention of projections, nonvoters were asked this open-ended question: "What would you say was the main reason you did not vote today?" Over two-thirds cited various priorities, obstacles, and inconveniences that "prevented" them from casting a ballot. Many (28 percent) said they were just "too busy," there were "not enough hours in the day" or they had "other commitments." Along with mostly general references to work, errands, and "kids," more varied answers included a honeymoon, a late-day plumbing mess, someone waiting in vain for an overseas telephone call, and a man who said he got out of jail (misdemeanor) too late in the day to cast a ballot.

Another sizable group (21 percent) consisted of those who were too sick or too tired, or whose spouse, child, parent, or friend was ill. Some nonvoters (7 percent) were out of town during the day or were still out of town, according to either a housemate or the follow-up survey of those who were not reached on election night. Some people had to work late (5 percent), or had car or other transportation problems (4 percent). Others had injuries or other physical handicaps that made them limit nonessential travel (1 percent) (see Table 4.2).

A few (0.4 percent) decided that they were too busy when they saw "long lines" outside the polling stations. A few others said they had to host out-of-town guests (0.3 percent), or contend with a recent death in the family (0.3 percent). Two women said they were in the late stages of pregnancy (0.3 percent). Two men said they "went fishing" (0.3 percent) and seemed to be sincere, not making a wisecrack. In the political vernacular, "going fishing" is a metaphor for abstaining, but some people really do go fishing on election day.

An obstacle cited by several people (1 percent) was that bad weather had kept them from voting, an initially mystifying excuse. The day was cool, suitable for a light jacket, but not cold. The sky was partly cloudy, but not stormy or rainy, although a light mist may have fallen early in the afternoon. Inspection revealed that those citing this reason were over the age of sixty-five and thus might have had reason to be hypercautious about avoiding slippery sidewalks and highways.

Table 4.2   Main Reason Cited for Not Voting

Obstacles/inconvenience/ other priorities (68.5%)			*Impact factors* (7.6%)	
			Result decided long ago	5.5
Busy; other commitment	27.5		One vote doesn't matter	2.1
Illness; weak/tired	20.7			
Out of town	6.7		*Alienation* (5.1%)	
Had to work late	5.3		Dislike the candidates	3.6
Transportation problems	4.1		Never vote	0.9
Bad weather	1.3		Don't like "the system"	0.6
Physical handicap	1.3			
Long lines	0.4		*Projections* (2.2%)	
Pregnant	0.3		TV projected winner	2.2
Death in family	0.3			
Guests visiting	0.3		*Miscellaneous* (2.8%)	
Fishing	0.3		Claim unregistered	1.8
			Would cancel spouse	0.6
Unmotivated/apathetic (8.3%)			Religious reason	0.4
Don't care who wins	4.3			
Too uninformed	3.0		*Vague* (5.5%)	
Feel lazy, apathetic	0.7		"Just didn't"	3.6
Undecided on candidates	0.3		Refused to say	1.0
			"Personal reasons"	0.9

Note: Total (n = 676) is based on 639 from the election night survey plus 37 from the follow-up survey.

In the apathetic grouping fell the 8 percent of nonvoters who did not seem to have sufficient energy or motivation to get themselves to the polls. Some (4 percent) dismissed the election with indifference ("I don't care who wins"), or admitted they were too lazy to bother voting (1 percent). Others (3 percent) confessed they had not followed the election and felt too uninformed to vote. A couple of people (0.3 percent) said they had "just not gotten around to deciding" for whom to vote.

Some degree of alienation characterized at least 5 percent of the nonvoters. They were not indifferent to or bored by the election; they were bitter about it. A few were antagonistic toward "the system" (1 percent) or insisted they "never vote" (1 percent), but more were hostile toward the candidacies of both Walter Mondale and Ronald Reagan (4 percent).

Without making any reference to projections, some nonvoters (8 percent) raised issues of impact. Some (2 percent) voiced the refrain that "my one vote doesn't matter." Others (6 percent) said they did not bother to vote because "the results were decided days/weeks/months ago" and thus reflected a campaign manager's nightmare that supporters might not vote because their candidate looks like an easy winner or a hopeless loser.

Assorted miscellaneous explanations were voiced by 3 percent of the nonvoters. Some erroneously said they were not registered to vote (2 percent). A few (0.6 percent) said their spouses would cancel their vote, so neither had voted (or at least that is what the respondent believed). Three (0.4 percent) cited religious reasons.

In the "vague/unknown" category (6 percent) were those who would not or could not offer any particular reason for skipping the election. Some could not be cajoled to say anything beyond "just didn't" (4 percent) or "personal reasons" (1 percent). Also, a few (1 percent) refused—politely since this was Oregon ("Sorry, but I'd really rather not say.").

Television projections were blamed as the reason for not voting by 2.2 percent of the nonvoters surveyed. While they constituted only 15 out of the 676 nonvoters, they will be considered in more detail below.

Nonvoters Who Blamed Projections

Measurement Validity

About one out of fifty known nonvoters blamed network projections. Were they being candid? Official records can be used for concurrent validation of whether respondents are registered and voted. However, there is no reasonable way to verify answers to the question of why people did not vote. This is an inescapably foggy realm.

Whenever respondents are asked to identify their motivation for doing something, the quality of their answers depends on whether they (1) really do know clearly why they behaved as they did and (2) are willing to admit the reason or reasons to an interviewer. Their answers have validity only to the extent they can articulate their true motivations and choose to do so. Timeliness helps. Answers are more likely to be accurate while memories of events are still fresh. But timeliness does not totally solve the issues of self-awareness and candor.

Regarding self-awareness, some deep-seated explanations will probably never be articulated. A nonvoter is unlikely to say, "My civic engagement is minimized by my lack of social networks and my unfortunate adolescent socialization experiences." In contrast, projection news at least has the advantage of being a specific tangible event that transpired a few hours before the interview. If that news decisively changed voting plans, then it ought to be fairly memorable. Candor may be the larger problem.

Explanations asserted for not voting ranged from those that sounded highly convincing (e.g., not wanting to go into labor in a polling booth, a death in the immediate family, or a genuine office crisis requiring unexpected late work) to those that sometimes sounded more like excuses to avoid confessing complacency ("well, I guess I was pretty busy today"). Blaming external factors has the advantage of leaving the nonvoter innocent of dereliction of civic duties.

For this purpose, network anchormen should make excellent villains and projections a tempting excuse for someone who lacked the drive to vote. It is reasonable to be suspicious that, at least for some nonvoters, projections may have served as more of a rationalization than a motivation for not voting. If so, the small proportion blaming projections (2.2 percent of nonvoters) may be inflated to some unknown degree.

Statistical Implications

Inflated or not, with a random sample of 676 nonvoters at the 95 percent level of probability, confidence intervals around 2.2 percent are ±1.1 percent. In other words, extrapolating from this random sample of nonvoters, nineteen times out of twenty (i.e., the 95 percent probability level), the true percentage of those blaming projections in the entire population of nonvoters who were registered in this part of Oregon should fall between 1.1 percent and 3.3 percent.

This result is in line with prior academic surveys reviewed in Chapter 2. Out of the total of 654 nonvoters in those five surveys, 12 blamed projections. Out of the 676 nonvoters in this study, 15 blamed projections.[9]

Is 2.2 percent of nonvoters a lot or a little? It is a smaller percentage than critics expected, but a tiny turnout shift can still swing a close election. What share does 2.2 percent of nonvoters constitute out of the whole registered electorate? Official records show that 79 percent of all those who were registered voted, but such numbers are always distorted to some degree by outdated lists. An investigation of the registration records figured the true turnout of registered voters at between 88 and

92 percent.[10] Using the midpoint of 90 percent voting, if nonvoters were 10 percent of those eligible to vote, the 2.2 percent (±1.1 percent) of nonvoters who blamed projections would represent 0.22 percent (±0.11) of the all valid registered voters.

One-fifth of one percent sounds like a minuscule amount but it translates into a few hundred people in the First District of Oregon—perhaps as many as 956 (0.33 percent) or as few as 319 people (0.11 percent). The midrange estimate, based on 0.22 percent blaming projections, would be 637 people.[11] Assuming that the announcement of Reagan's victory was truly the "main reason" for not voting, whether a few hundred nonvoters could swing an election would depend on the extent to which they would have voted disproportionately for a particular candidate.[12]

Despite Reagan carrying Oregon and Republicans targeting his district, Democratic congressman Les AuCoin did win reelection, with 53 percent of the votes and a margin of 16,146 votes out of 260,667 cast. Did projections dampen turnout and shift its composition in a way that narrowed AuCoin's victory to any degree? Extrapolating to the entire district, a 0.22 percent decline in total turnout might have decreased total turnout by a few hundred votes. The (unknown) net preferences of those few hundred nonvoters would determine exactly how much their loss hurt or helped AuCoin's margin.

Summary

Despite three hours for its dissemination, the exceptionally early projection news only reached about half of those eligible to vote. That news did not drive thousands of discouraged Democrats and/or bored Republicans from the polls in eastern Oregon. Nine out of ten people who were registered to vote went to the polls on that election day. Among those who did not cast a ballot, only 2.2 percent blamed projections; they represented approximately 0.22 percent of all those confirmed as genuinely eligible to vote.

These data are consistent with results from the other surveys that asked the reason for not voting (see Chapter 2). With a preexisting likelihood of voting or not voting, established by a lifetime of influences, few nonvoters claimed to be swayed by projections.

Without any reasonable way to verify a nonvoter's claim that "projections made me do it," the existence or extent of exaggeration remains unknown. However, in the chapters that follow, research is reported using other methodologies that do not rely on nonvoters' reports of their motivations. Other locations and other elections will also be examined to see if they corroborate the survey findings presented here.

Notes

1. Part of this argument's appeal is that it might explain the anomalous findings of a substantial projection impact in 1980. An alternative explanation was that Jimmy Carter's early concession speech on-camera (by itself or in combination with projections) accounted for effects found in 1980. However, Chapter 2 noted methodology problems, including the misleading California registration data, that accounted for a good share of the peculiarities in studies of 1980.

2. In 1984, for several reasons—including pollsters' "failure to detect Reagan's big victory in 1980," Mondale's frequent attacks on polls, and considerable variability in polls throughout the 1984 campaign (Kohut, 1986, p. 2)—the election outcome was not obvious to half of the citizenry. This was not unusual. In only one presidential election between 1952 and 2000 did a majority (and it was a small majority of 56 percent in 1972) tell NES interviewers that they believed that one candidate would win by "quite a bit." Even in 1996, when preelection surveys showed Bill Clinton crushing Bob Dole (the CBS/*New York Times* poll gave Clinton an 18 percent point margin), the public did not anticipate a landslide; a majority (53 percent and thus obviously not all Dole supporters) told NES interviewers that they expected a close contest.

3. Despite repeated calls, there was no answer at 177 telephone numbers that evening. A follow-up survey found 37 who said they were out of town. See endnote 10 for a summary of the follow-up study of listed nonvoters who could not be contacted on election night.

4. Whether people vote is a matter of public record, but interviewers should not tell nonvoters ominously, "We know you didn't vote today." Instead, an intentionally loaded question was used to try to make it easier for people to admit not voting. Such questions are considered justified when respondents might otherwise be reluctant to answer candidly. The question was worded as follows: "We're finding that lots of people did not vote today because they just didn't have a chance or for some other reason. Were you one of the people who did not go to the polls today?"

5. Most callers in Oregon were volunteers who, like many westerners, disliked early projections and hoped they were contributing to solid research that would document the damage done by projections. They are identified and thanked, along with callers from George Washington University, in this book's Acknowledgments.

6. A subsequent follow-up survey added thirty-seven nonvoters who were out of town on election day and night.

7. This difference between voters and nonvoters (who are registered to vote) is statistically significant with a chi-square test at the .0001 level of probability, meaning there is less than 1 chance in 10,000 that such a difference might have been produced by chance variation in random sampling.

8. Due to the addition of nonvoters who were out of town and did not participate in the initial election night survey, percentages in Table 4.2 have some fractions that differ slightly from those reported in "Early Projections in 1984: How Western Voters Deplored but Ignored Them," a paper presented to the American Association of Public Opinion Research on May 18, 1985.

9. The percentage blaming projections in metro Portland was a bit higher than the median of prior studies, but the difference is not statistically significant; confidence intervals around 2.2 percent (±1.1 percent) overlap with the survey result summarized in Chapter 2.

10. To measure the inflation error in these registration lists, three representative precincts that were among those intensively surveyed on election night were selected for extensive follow-up analysis. Of the 1,656 names registered in these precincts, records showed that 1,315 had voted—a 79.4 percent turnout of listed registered voters. (This almost perfectly echoed the total turnout of 79.3 percent in Multnomah, Washington, and Yamhill Counties, where 427,540 voted out of 539,078 on the rolls.) Of the 341 "nonvoters" in these three precincts, 122 could be verified as living in the precinct on election day (either because they were interviewed on election night in the survey of nonvoters or because they were eventually verified in subsequent calls to their address); 157 had definitely moved; and 62 could not be verified. Consequently, the true turnout of valid registered voters in this part of Oregon in this election was somewhere between 88 percent [1315 / (1656 − 157)] if all unverifieds were living in the precinct and 92 percent [1315 / (1656 − 157 − 62)] if all unverifieds were invalid. Remember that this high participation rate is based strictly on those who are registered to vote—not on estimates of the entire "voting-age population."

11. Assuming the ratio of voters to valid nonvoters reported in note 10, based on its 260,667 voters in the 1984 general election, the congressional district would have had approximately 289,630 valid registered voters. If they constituted 0.22 percent of that total, 637 nonvoters blamed projections for not voting.

12. Who were these 15 nonvoters (out of 676) who said projection news was the "main reason" they did not vote? Of course, this subsample is much too small to provide any generalizable data. Out of curiosity rather than academic rigor, it was hard to resist peeking at their political and demographic characteristics. Upon inspection, they did not appear to be an especially distinctive group. This small band of people at the heart of so much controversy did not vary much from other nonvoters by age, education, or sex (eight

women and seven men). This part of Oregon leaned toward the Democrats and these 15 discouraged voters were more likely to be Democrats (9) than Republicans (3) or Independents (3). Yet thanks to a "Reagan Democrat," their votes, if they had they voted, would not have been too far off from district patterns. They would have divided between Democrat Walter Mondale (8) and Ronald Reagan (7) for president, and between Democrat Margie Hendricksen (8) and Mark Hatfield (7) for senator, and gone for Democrat Les AuCoin (9) over Bill Moshofsky (6) for the U.S. House.

5

Turnout Test
of Twin Counties:
Eastern Oregon

Some comparisons are so dissimilar (such as West Coast versus East Coast turnout) that—even with perfect measures—any turnout differences could be due to dozens of possible explanations. Comparison groups that are more closely matched help rule out those alternative explanations. That is why controlled experiments where groups are matched using random assignment are so powerful. If the only real difference between two groups is whether or not they were given a vaccine, then differences in the subsequent health of the two groups can be attributed to the vaccine.[1]

For projection research, a true controlled field experiment is not feasible. Can one reasonably be approximated? The closest possible match would be a within-state comparison of two places that have similar demographics, identical registration and voting laws, and even similar ballots—but that differ in the volume of exposure to projections. Eastern Oregon in the 1980s offered just such an opportunity worthy of being called a "natural experiment."

Malheur and Grant Counties

In November, all of Oregon uses Pacific standard time, except one county in the far eastern part of the state: Malheur County uses mountain standard time (see Figure 5.1). Polls close in Oregon at 8:00 P.M. in each time zone, so Malheur's polls close one hour earlier than in the rest of Oregon. As a result, Malheur is exposed to one less hour of early

Figure 5.1   Matched Oregon Counties

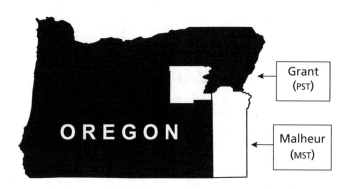

network projections. If projections discourage voting, then neighboring counties, if they are similar in other respects, should have proportionately fewer people voting at the end of the day than does Malheur.

Residents of neighboring Grant County were in the same TV market and were very similar demographically to residents of Malheur County. No two jurisdictions are ever identical, but these two were remarkably alike. They were almost indistinguishable on many demographic factors known to predict voter turnout, such as education, age, race, occupational types, mobility, and rural-urban status (see Table 5.1).

Census Bureau data showed Grant and Malheur to have been equally urban (43 percent each) and to have had similar growth rates (15–16 percent), equal proportions of citizens over the age of sixty-five (12 percent each), similar median ages (thirty-two and thirty), few African American residents (fewer than 1 percent each), and nearly the same shares of college (11–12 percent) and high school graduates (71–68 percent). Also, employment in the two counties was distributed into the same general categories; manufacturing and other industries were not markedly more important in one county than in the other.

Economically, the two counties were fairly close, as indicated by median per capita income and other measures. In Malheur, 11 percent of the households made over $30,000 annually, while in Grant the share was 13 percent. Compared to Malheur, Grant had slightly fewer poor households and slightly higher median per capita income.

Table 5.1   Comparison of Malheur and Grant Counties

	Malheur (MST)	Grant (PST)
Age		
Median age	30	32
Age 65 and older (%)	12	12
Age 5 to 17 years (%)	23	21
Education		
High school or more (%)	68	71
College or more (%)	12	11
Civilian employment		
Manufacturing (%)	11	15
Retail trade (%)	21	18
Professional (%)	19	17
Other industry (%)	23	25
Income		
Households < $10,000 (%)	38	32
Households > $30,000 (%)	11	13
Median per capita ($)	7,776	8,442
Other		
Urban population (%)	43	43
Growth 1970–1980 (%)	16	15
Black population (%)	0.4	0.0

Source: City and County Data Book (Census Bureau, 1983).

Not only were the two counties demographically quite similar, but their ballots were nearly identical in 1984. In both counties, voters had the same choices for president and vice president, U.S. senator, U.S. representative, state treasurer, secretary of state, attorney general, state supreme court judge, state senator, and nine statewide referenda. Ballots differed only with respect to district attorney and state representative, but the two incumbent district attorneys had no opponents, and the two incumbent Republican state representatives were both easily re-elected. These ballot similarities are important because, if one of the counties had more hotly contested races, that factor alone could account for minor differences in turnout.

To learn if turnout declined after projections were broadcast, it would be necessary to track the times that ballots were cast throughout the day. The outstanding cooperation of the two county clerks—Carol

Voigt of Canyon City (Grant) and Robert Markham of Vale (Malheur)—made just such a detailed investigation possible. Voigt and Markham agreed to participate because, like most Oregonians, they disliked the practice of early calls and hoped the findings could be used to attack the practice. They instructed their precinct officials to mark carefully (on forms supplied by the author) the time of day, in half-hour intervals, when every vote was cast. Together, the two counties provided data on the time of day when almost 15,000 people voted.

The records were meticulously kept. Precinct officials accounted for the voting times of all but two votes officially cast in Grant County (99.95 percent); data from the Malheur precincts were also quite thorough (99.94 percent recorded).[2] This detailed information made it possible to track whether late-day turnout in Grant County (exposed to an extra hour of projections) was lower than turnout in Malheur County.

Pacific vs. Mountain Turnout

On the same day with the same weather in the same state, two very similar populations were faced with very similar ballots, but those living in Malheur had just concluded the heavy voting hour of 5:00–6:00, when projections began, unlike their time-lagged neighbors, who were just getting off work at 5:00 when projections hit. If projections depress turnout, PST Grant should have had lower turnout than MST Malheur. Their actual differences were in the opposite direction.

Total turnout of registered voters in PST Grant (72.1 percent) was *higher* than that in MST Malheur (68.2 percent). Higher turnout in Grant is noteworthy, but it does not, by itself, negate the chance that its turnout was still suppressed somewhat by early TV calls. Despite close matching, the 3.9 percent turnout gap might still be due to other factors, such as the slight difference in economic status or differences in how registration lists were kept.

One advantage of using hourly turnout records is that such factors can be controlled by calculating hourly turnout as a proportion of all votes cast. This allows a comparison of late-day turnout to the number of ballots that were cast in the morning and early afternoon, instead of a comparison to registration lists. This avoids the risk that the two lists, even though they are under the same state laws, were not maintained with exactly the same vigor. So, ignoring the 3.9 percentage point higher turnout of listed registered voters in Grant (with more exposure to projections), what happened late in the day, holding total turnout constant?

Figure 5.2 shows the cumulative hourly turnout in Grant and Malheur as a percentage of all those voting. Proportionately, residents of Grant voted just slightly more in the morning and a bit less in the early afternoon. Overall, as might be expected for two closely matched counties, patterns were quite similar, but the central issue is late-day turnout.

Despite its extra hour of projections at the start of the postwork rush, PST Grant had a higher proportion of its votes cast between 5:00 and 8:00 P.M. than did MST Malheur (see Figure 5.3). Grant had 32 percent of its ballots cast in that period compared to 31 percent in Malheur (where projections did not begin until 6:00 local time). While late-day turnout in Malheur during the last two hours took a slight lead (19 percent versus 18 percent), that slim margin vanished during the last hour.

Figure 5.2   Cumulative Hourly Turnout as a Percentage of All Votes Cast

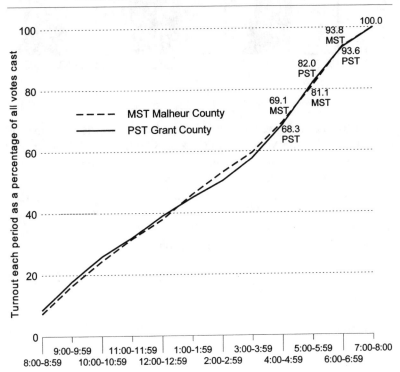

Figure 5.3   Late-Day Hourly Turnout as a Percentage of All Votes Cast

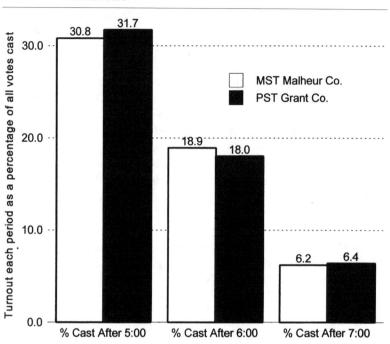

Grant had slightly more votes cast from 7:00 to 8:00 (its third hour of projections) than did Malheur from 7:00 to 8:00 (its second hour of projections). Despite more exposure to projections, Grant County had comparatively higher late-day voting than did Malheur County.

These data on the behavior of almost 15,000 voters can be calculated several ways (see Table 5.2), but in each instance the results are the same: overall late-day turnout did not suffer in the county where voters had more exposure to TV projections.[3]

Daylight and Turnout

Are there any other factors that might have inflated late-day turnout in Grant or depressed it in Malheur, thus masking the effects of TV projections at the end of the day? Could daylight or weather be such a factor?

Table 5.2   Late-Day Hourly Turnout in Oregon's Malheur and
Grant Counties

	Turnout as a Percentage . . .					
	Of All Registered Voters		Of All Those Registered But Not Yet Voted		Of All Votes Cast	
	Malheur (MST)	Grant (PST)	Malheur (MST)	Grant (PST)	Malheur (MST)	Grant (PST)
Before 5:00 P.M.	47.1	49.3	47.1	49.3	69.1	68.3
5:00–5:59 P.M.	8.2	9.9	15.4	19.4	12.0	13.7
6:00–6:59 P.M.	8.7	8.3	19.4	20.3	12.7	11.6
7:00–8:00 P.M.	4.2	4.6	11.6	14.1	6.2	6.4

On November 6, 1984, the eastern Oregon sky was partly cloudy in both counties. Local temperatures were in the forties throughout the day and early evening. While the counties' weather did not vary, the amount of late-day sunshine did. The sun set that day at 5:35 P.M. MST and 4:35 P.M. PST. Consequently, it was still light at 5:00 in the afternoon in Vale (MST Malheur's county seat), but it was dark eighty miles to the west in Canyon City (PST Grant's county seat) one hour later when the clock read 5:00 there.

If the earlier nightfall has any impact, it ought to reduce turnout in the county with less late afternoon sunshine. This factor ought to work to the advantage of Malheur and to the disadvantage of Grant. Nevertheless, citizens of Grant had both an hour more of darkness *and* an hour more to hear TV projections, but they still turned out to vote at slightly higher rates at day's end than did their cohorts in Malheur.

1988 and Beyond

Projections were broadcast later in 1988: 6:17 P.M. PST by CBS, 6:21 by ABC, and 7:30 by NBC, this time declaring that Vice President George Bush had beaten Governor Michael Dukakis. Potential voters in Grant County could have heard projections on CBS as early as one hour and forty-three minutes before the polls closed in 1988 compared to a maximum of forty-three minutes in Malheur.

In 1988, the ballots in the two counties were still quite similar. Detailed tracking of hourly voting rates is not available for 1988, but countywide totals are available. Once again, the PST county with the extra dose of projections (Grant) had slightly higher voter turnout than the matched MST county (Malheur). Turnout in Grant was 82.4 percent of all registered voters, compared to a turnout of 80.2 percent in Malheur.

In the 1990s, voting by mail became popular in Oregon and, demographically, the two counties increasingly began to differ. In 1998, voters in Oregon overwhelmingly endorsed a ballot measure to switch entirely to a vote-by-mail system. Most ballots are returned prior to election day, but those on election day must be returned to designated locations by 8:00 P.M.; thus the new system drastically minimizes the possibility of projection effects.

The 7:00–8:00 Decline

Western poll workers have sometimes complained that turnout begins to dwindle dramatically soon after televised projections. In their eyes, this sequence looks like cause and effect. The polls often seemed especially empty during the final hour after projections—instead of climaxing with a steady stream of last-minute voters much like taxpayer lines at a post office before midnight on April 15.

Election clerks have supplied the wrong interpretation to correct observations. Turnout will almost always be less after projections are announced than immediately before—but not because of projections. Turnout in the West declines sharply near the end of the day with or without projections.

First, consider the evidence from eastern Oregon. Following the after-work rush and entering the dinner hour, turnout plummeted in both counties during the last hour polls were open (7:00–8:00 P.M.). The decline was not a function of what was happening on television but a function of daily rhythms of work and meals in each time zone. When Malheur turnout plunged to 6.2 percent during its final hour, Grant's turnout did not. The "dinnertime drop-off" did not hit Grant until the next hour, when 7:00 arrived in the Pacific time zone. Only then did its turnout fall sharply, to 6.4 percent.

A second set of evidence comes from a large California project (Fuchs and Becker, 1968). Election clerks in 2,152 diverse precincts in Alameda County recorded the time of day that 192,867 Californians voted in the 1966 election (which featured Ronald Reagan's 1 million–vote upset of the incumbent Democrat, Governor Pat Brown). In that off-year, projection-free California gubernatorial election, turnout of those voting fell from 13.7 percent of those voting (5:00–6:00) to 10.7 percent (6:00–7:00) and then shrank to 4.4 percent in the final hour (7:00–8:00).

A third and even more extensive body of data (Los Angeles, 1974–2002) is analyzed in Chapter 7 and confirms the 7:00–8:00 turnout collapse, with or without projections, in both presidential and off-year elections. This explains why election officials are always likely to see a sizable decline in turnout following projections, with the final hour slowing to a trickle compared to the 5:00 postwork flood. To poll workers, the subsequent postprojection decline is interpreted as powerful proof of causality (the classic *post hoc ergo propter hoc* fallacy), but the same thing happens without projections.

Summary

In a natural experiment based on the comparative late-day behavior of two closely matched Oregon counties, no evidence was found that projections discouraged voting at all. Grant was hit with projections at 5:00 P.M. PST as people were getting off work, but had more of its votes cast during the last three hours than did its "twin" MST county, Malheur, where it was 6:00 P.M. local time when projections began. A few nonvoters in the Portland-area study (Chapter 4) blamed projections, but such people were undetectable here.

Notes

1. True randomized field experiments tend to be less feasible for social science than in medical research. One example of a true field experiment in political communications is William Adams and Dennis Smith's test (1980) of the impact of get-out-the-vote telephone calls on voter turnout. "Lab" experiments are considerably easier to conduct (especially using college sophomores, instead of the general public). For example, many dozens of lab experiments have been published regarding the impact of negative campaign advertisements (Lau et al., 1999).

2. Some maps assign all of Malheur to mountain time. In fact, far from the population centers of this expansive county, Pacific time is used in a sparsely

populated section of the far southern end of Malheur, described as a semidesert area with a few steep mountains. Data from that precinct were not included; and for simplicity, Malheur is described here as a mountain time county, which it overwhelmingly is.

3. If one is willing to make the assumption of equally precise registration records in the two counties, turnout can be calculated as a percentage of all registered voters. At the minute projections began, turnout of all registered voters was 2.1 percentage points higher in Grant. By the end of its first hour of projection news, turnout in Grant had grown to 3.8 percentage points higher than that of Malheur (where the corresponding 5:00 hour of voting lacked projection news). When the polls closed, Grant's lead was 3.9 percent. (Because the Malheur and Grant data are comprehensive rather than random samples, inferential statistics such as confidence intervals and significance tests are not required here.)

6

Heartland Not Disheartened: Idaho, Kansas, and North Dakota

The previous two chapters presented data from the state of Oregon. Are the findings unique to that state? The generalizability (external validity) of the findings can be tested by studying other states. At the same time, it remains important to examine closely matched jurisdictions for comparisons that (for internal validity) help rule out alternative explanations.

As shown in Chapter 5, matching can be improved by comparing turnout within a single state that has similar counties in two time zones, instead of comparing different states (e.g., California versus New York) or different regions. Among the states where polls were open at least one hour after the earliest 1984 projection, five states spanning two time zones closed their western polls one hour after closing most eastern polls—Texas, Oregon, Kansas, Idaho, and North Dakota. Texas lacked any close match for El Paso,[1] its far-western MST outpost, and Oregon was the site for the two previous chapters. The remaining three suitable states are Kansas, Idaho, and North Dakota. This chapter turns first to Kansas and Idaho, then to the more difficult case of North Dakota.

Time Zone Comparisons

In Kansas, five far-western counties used mountain standard time,[2] while the hundred other counties were in the central time zone. Most Kansas polls closed at 7:00 P.M. CST or MST.[3] In Idaho, the boundary runs north to south instead of east to west. The ten northern counties of the Idaho panhandle were on Pacific standard time, while the thirty-four southern counties were on mountain standard time. Idaho polls close at 8:00 P.M. MST or PST.

What is the best way to take advantage of these intrastate time zones? A crude approach is to compare the turnout for the entire parts of the states in each time zone, a method that would produce terrible comparisons in both states. The rural, western MST edge of Kansas is a poor match for the less rural, more affluent remainder of the state, which has cities like Topeka, Wichita, and Kansas City, and college towns like Manhattan and Lawrence. Likewise, it makes little sense to compare the whole PST Idaho panhandle with MST southern Idaho. The economy, demographics, and Democratic politics of northern Idaho differ substantially from the economy, demographics, and Republican politics of heavily Mormon southern Idaho.

As was the case in eastern Oregon, a better comparison can be constructed by finding similar neighboring counties on either side of the time zone line. This works in Kansas and Idaho because, in both states, adjacent counties by the time zone boundary happen to be fairly similar.

For Kansas, the five MST western counties were paired with five CST counties to the east, immediately on the other side of the time zone boundary but still a part of the Great Plains. Their names and locations are shown in Figure 6.1.[4] The two sets of Kansas counties were extremely similar in terms of the age, income, education, race, occupations, and politics of their residents (see Table 6.1). The paired counties were all in the same congressional district. The only ballot difference was that more MST counties were in uncontested or uncompetitive state senatorial or state representative districts, perhaps a mild disincentive to vote compared to the ballots in the CST comparison counties.

In the state of Idaho, the large county of Idaho spans the width of the state and sits atop the PST side of the time zone boundary. Technically, the time zone cuts a few miles inside part of the county, but precinct polling places are in the PST bulk of the county. Idaho County had much in common with the two adjoining MST counties to the south, Lemhi and Valley,[5] especially in terms of age distribution, growth rate, urban-rural status, race, and politics. Compared to the PST county, the MST counties had relatively fewer manufacturing jobs and slightly higher education levels, but income distributions were not too far apart. Ballots in all three counties were identical except that Lemhi was in the

Figure 6.1   Matched Idaho and Kansas Counties

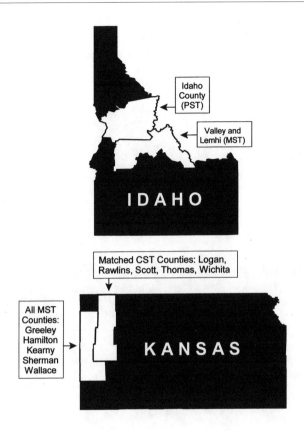

congressional district of George Hansen, an incumbent under indict-
ment (later incarcerated) who lost his seat by a mere 170 votes. This
closely fought race should have added a stimulus to vote on Lemhi's
"early" side of the time line. To the extent that the Kansas and Idaho
matches vary, the known turnout advantages favored the earlier time
zone with a slight edge in education, more competition on the ballot,
and, in Kansas, some extra daylight. Thus, any unavoidable "selection
bias" leaned toward higher turnout in earlier zones.

Another issue is that without hourly turnout data, voter participation here is calculated from voter registration lists, usually a messy approach because lists are inflated with the names of people who have

Table 6.1   Similarity of Matched Comparison Counties

	Kansas		Idaho	
	Five MST Counties	Five CST Counties	Idaho County (PST)	Lemhi and Valley (MST)
Age				
Median age	31	31	30	30
Age 65 and older (%)	13	14	13	11
Age 5 to 17 years (%)	22	21	23	22
Education				
High school or more (%)	71	71	69	75
College or more (%)	12	14	12	16
Civilian employment				
Manufacturing (%)	4	4	17	9
Retail trade (%)	23	23	18	23
Professional (%)	21	20	15	18
Other industry (%)	26	26	23	20
Income				
Households <$10,000 (%)	31	33	32	31
Households >$30,000 (%)	13	14	12	12
Median per capita ($)	6,443	6,531	5,873	6,015
Other				
Urban population (%)	33	39	25	25
Growth 1970–1980 (%)	–1	–1	5	5
Black population (%)	0.2	0.1	0.0	0.0
1980 Reagan vote (%)	68	71	63	67

Sources: City and County Data Book (Census Bureau, 1983) and *David Leip's Atlas of U.S. Presidential Elections* (http://uselectionatlas.org).

died or moved. However, this use of registration totals to calculate turnout should not be quite as risky as relying on registration lists over time and across states, for three reasons:

1. Comparison counties were governed by the same state election laws and regulations for registration records. While rules were not necessarily applied with equal rigor in every county, at least they were operating under the same rules, something most cross-state comparisons lack.
2. The comparison is for a single election and is not threatened by changes in registration policies over time.

3. Since these areas had stable populations and were not faced with a large influx of new residents, maintaining registration records should not have been too onerous. In the prior decade, these Kansas counties lost 1 percent of their residents, while the Idaho counties gained just 5 percent.

Together, these three factors mitigate but do not eliminate concerns about the reliance on registration totals (in the absence of hourly turnout figures). Be that as it may, what did the turnout records show? Despite the slightly less educated population, a little less competition in races for the state legislature, darker skies—and the extra hour of exposure to early TV projections—turnout appears to have been slightly *higher* in the later time zones.

Voter Turnout in Kansas and Idaho

The Kansas CST counties had just closed their polls (7:00 P.M.) in 1984 when CBS declared Ronald Reagan victorious over Walter Mondale. Meanwhile, citizens in adjacent MST counties continued to cast ballots for another hour while projections were repeatedly broadcast. (CBS was soon joined by ABC and NBC.)

If projections discourage voting, turnout should have been lower in the five projection-exposed, western counties of Kansas. That was not the case. Turnout of registered voters was 78.2 percent in the five MST counties subject to projections,[6] surpassing the 77.5 percent turnout in the five matched CST counties that concluded voting before projections were broadcast.

The result was the same in Idaho. Turnout was slightly higher where there was an extra hour of projection news. The PST county's final turnout of registered voters was 74.2 percent, exceeding the 73.7 percent turnout in the MST counties.

Caveats

This study falls short of approximating a "natural experiment." It can be termed a "static group design" because, although its groups are tolerably matched, there are fewer "formal means of certifying that the groups would have been equivalent had it not been for the X" (Campbell and Stanley, 1963, p. 12). To be sure, many studies are conducted using less-than-dazzling comparisons. Rough comparisons are not so troublesome when the effects studied are large ones[7]—but identifying very small effects amid the noise and clutter of uneven comparisons may be impossible.[8]

With the Kansas and Idaho comparisons, one has to worry that small effects may be submerged by county variation in registration record-keeping.[9] In both states, comparison counties also appeared slightly tilted (by economics and competitive local races) toward lower turnout in counties getting more projection news. However, because the outcomes were in the opposite direction, it can be argued that these factors lend the findings more credence. Despite those slight disadvantages and despite projections, the more projection-exposed counties had a higher turnout of registered voters.

North Dakota

As the sole U.S. state without voter registration, North Dakota is not an easy place to make turnout comparisons.[10] Turnout rates must be calculated based on estimates of the voting-age population by county in 1984.[11]

One comparison group consisted of the ten counties in the mountain time zone,[12] all of which closed their polling stations at 7:00 P.M. The central time zone comparison group consisted of all counties remaining after excluding counties that straddled two time zones,[13] that had variable poll closing times,[14] or that are located in the Red River Valley and adjoining eastern plains,[15] where the geography, history, demographics, and politics are distinct from the western side of the state. A dozen CST counties composed the resulting comparison group.[16]

Polls closed in the twelve CST counties before projections began, while in the ten MST counties, prospective voters could have been exposed to projections as early as one hour before their polls closed (7:00 P.M. MST). Again, no evidence was found that projections dampened turnout. Projection-exposed counties achieved a 63.7 percent turnout rate, while the comparison counties recorded a fraction less, 63.6 percent.

By itself, not too much should be made of this North Dakota finding. It does again show a continued absence of any yawning chasm in
turnout rates on either side of time zone, projection-exposure boundaries. However, given the inexact estimates of voting-age population,
these findings should not carry any weight as to whether there are more
subtle projection effects.

Later Elections and Summary

In Kansas and North Dakota, 1984 was the last election in the century
when their MST counties were exposed to projections before polls
closed. In Idaho, the comparison was still feasible in 1988, when maximum exposure was one hour and forty-three minutes PST or forty-three
minutes MST. Turnout was again higher (5 percent) in the more projection-exposed county. In 1992, projections aired just minutes before
polls closed, and by 1996, voting-by-mail and demographic shifts had
begun to confound the Idaho comparison. In 2000 and 2004, the networks did not name the next president before the polls closed.

What have the findings in this chapter contributed to understanding if or how much projections decrease turnout? In three states, counties that were more exposed to projections had slightly *higher* turnout
rates of registered voters than did matched neighboring counties.
Known shortcomings in the matching should have helped turnout in the
less exposed counties in all three states, but they still showed slightly
lower turnout rates. Caution is in order because the findings in this one
chapter rely on turnout measured as a percentage of inflated registration lists (or estimated voting-age population), not an exact measure
even within the same state in the same year.

In isolation, these findings suggest that countywide projection exposure is not related to large declines in voter turnout, but the methodology is less persuasive regarding the chance that projections caused
small declines. Viewing these results not in isolation but as building on
the more rigorous study in Oregon (Chapter 5) gives them added
weight, because they consistently echo the identical Oregon pattern in
Kansas, Idaho, and North Dakota. To advance the analysis further, it
would be ideal to study additional elections, to explore evidence from
California, the colossus of the West, and to utilize yet another methodology. Those objectives are undertaken in Chapter 7.

Notes

1. El Paso in the far western MST tip of Texas has no nearby CST city even remotely comparable.

2. This sentence is in the past tense because in 1990 Kearny County switched entirely to the central time zone. A small eastern segment of the county was already on central time in 1984, but most polling precincts were in the mountain time zone.

3. In 1986, telephone calls to county clerks of the ten counties verified that all closed their polls at 7:00 P.M. in their respective time zones. A Kansas statute now prohibits MST counties from keeping polls open past 7:00 P.M., but that law only codified previous practice.

4. The only county to the immediate east of the MST counties that was not included in the CST comparison group was Finney, which was more urban and otherwise too different from the five rural and small town counties of MST Kansas. Rawlins, on the north edge of the matched counties, was substituted for Finney.

5. Adding counties farther north or south introduces large social and economic differences. Adams County, the only MST county contiguous to PST Idaho County that was not included, was more rural (97 percent) than the matched counties (each 75 percent rural).

6. Excluding Kearny County from the MST group (because it had a few precincts in the central zone) increases the turnout superiority of the more western counties, with a combined turnout of 79.1 percent in the remaining four MST counties.

7. For example, Wisconsin tried major welfare reforms in the early 1990s and its welfare rolls immediately began to plunge drastically (down over 90 percent). Before-and-after comparisons with adjacent states were so dramatic that analysts had little problem attributing the decline to the policy change (rather than to other differences between the states). That interpretation would not have been so persuasive if Wisconsin's welfare rolls had only declined a few percent.

8. This is not merely the problem of achieving "statistical significance" for small effects when samples are used. No statistical test solves the analytical problem of deciding the degree to which other factors can be ruled out as alternative explanations.

9. Some analysts might dismiss this potential problem by noting that county-to-county variation in inflated lists should be random and not systematically more inflated on one side of the time zone boundary than on the other. Conceivably, however, with only a few counties in each comparison group, random variation might leave the western groups with a little less list inflation (and the appearance of higher turnout) that might hide any small projection effects that lowered turnout. Concern about this possibility would be greater if the same results had not been obtained in four states—Idaho, Kansas, and

North Dakota (and eastern Oregon in the previous chapter)—thereby reducing the chances that measurement error alone produced this consistent pattern.

10. Election administration was extremely decentralized. Fifty-three county auditors had to be surveyed individually to obtain the following information: Most counties closed their 1984 polls at 7:00 P.M. asynchronously (7:00 CST and then 7:00 MST). Exceptions were counties with mixed closing times, often 8:00 or 9:00 in the city (e.g., Bismark, Fargo, Grand Forks) and 7:00 in rural precincts. Since available data were countywide, those five counties were excluded from the analysis.

11. These data were derived from the U.S. Census Bureau's 1984 population estimates and provided by Gary Goreham of the State Census Data Center at North Dakota State University.

12. In 1992, Oliver County shifted to the central time zone.

13. Dune, McKenzie, Morton, and Sioux.

14. Burleigh, Cass, Grand Forks, McKenzie, Morton, Sioux, Ward, and Williams.

15. All those counties to the east of and including Towner, Wells, Benson, Stutsman, Logan, and McIntosh.

16. The ten MST counties were Adams, Billings, Bowman, Grant, Golden Valley, Hettinger, Mercer, Oliver, Slope, and Stark. The twelve CST comparison counties were Bottineau, Burke, Divide, Emmons, Kidder, McHenry, McLean, Mountrail, Pierce, Renville, Rolette, and Sheridan.

7

Decades of Dinnertime Dropoff: California

Since 1974, the Office of the Registrar Recorder in Los Angeles County has tracked hourly voter turnout in thirty precincts that mirror the county rather well.[1] The result is a valuable body of data showing the time of day when hundreds of thousands of Californians voted in sixteen elections over the span of three decades.

The Los Angeles County hourly turnout data were originally released as percentages of all registered voters, a formula at the mercy of changing amounts of inflation in voter registration rolls and major regulatory changes (e.g., the 1993 National Voter Registration Act and California's 1978 abandonment of automatic purging, discussed in Chapter 2). The problem of inconsistently inflated lists can be avoided by recalculating hourly turnout as a percentage of all votes cast. Using this approach, the volume of invalid names on the registration list is irrelevant. Instead, late-day turnout is analyzed relative to turnout earlier in the day. The results will indicate whether a series of projected elections had relatively fewer late-day voters than did unprojected presidential elections.

Projected Elections

Figure 7.1 shows Los Angeles County turnout patterns for the three major projected elections when the winner was declared at least two hours before polls closed in California. Despite many dissimilarities in the 1980, 1984, and 1996 campaigns, patterns of turnout among those

Figure 7.1   Los Angeles County Turnout in Major Projected Elections

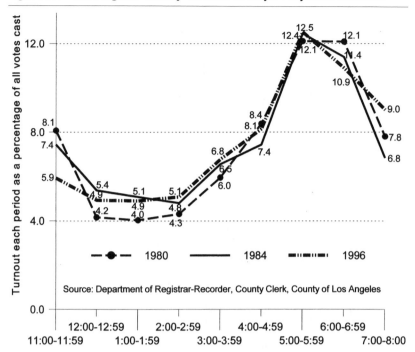

Source: Department of Registrar-Recorder, County Clerk, County of Los Angeles

who voted were remarkably similar in all three years. Each election day began with an early-morning push that drifted down to a slow midday pace (noon–3:00 P.M.), the least-busy period all day. Turnout then ramped up rapidly to crest during the 5:00–6:00 postwork rush hour. Voting remained at high levels during the 6:00–7:00 hour and declined sharply in the final hour.

In all three years, the presidential winner was projected between 5:00 and 6:01 P.M. PST, and without any comparisons, the ensuing decreases in voting look like the terrible aftermath of damaging projection effects. However, patterns from other years show that voter turnout routinely tumbles in the last hour, whether or not projections are aired.

Unprojected Elections

In Figure 7.2, the mean hourly turnout from the three elections projected early is contrasted with the opposite extreme, the cliffhanger

Figure 7.2   Los Angeles County Turnout in Projected vs. Unprojected Elections

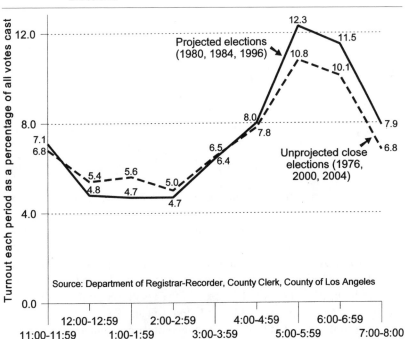

Source: Department of Registrar-Recorder, County Clerk, County of Los Angeles

elections of 2004,[2] 2000, and 1976,[3] when no nationwide winners were announced before polls closed in California. During the crucial late-day period, proportionately more people voted in the projected elections.

Going beyond mean trends in Figure 7.2, every projected election had comparatively more late voting than did any of the close elections (see Table 7.1). In 1980, 1984, and 1996, more votes were cast during the 6:00–8:00 period after projections were broadcast than during that same period in the close unprojected elections of 1976, 2000, and 2004.

1988 and 1992

In 1988, projections aired later, not until 6:17 (CBS), 6:21 (ABC), and 7:30 (NBC) P.M. PST. Consequently, the postprojection period to be tested is the final 7:00–8:00 hour of voting. Once again, relative turnout

Table 7.1   Los Angeles County 6:00–8:00 P.M. Turnout as a Percentage of All Votes Cast

Projected		Unprojected	
Elections (Projected 5:15–6:01)	Percentage Cast 6:00–8:00	Elections	Percentage Cast 6:00–8:00
1980	19.86	1976	17.41
1984	18.23	2000	18.00
1996	18.93	2004	17.49
Mean	19.00	Mean	17.62

was higher during the hour following the 1988 projections than it was during the unprojected elections (see Table 7.2).

No postprojection data are available for 1992 because network projections were announced just twelve minutes before polls closed on the West Coast. As an election that was very nearly not projected, 1992 fit the pattern of the two unprojected elections and had fewer late-day voters in the last two hours (14.5 percent) than occurred in the early projection elections of 1980, 1984, and 1996 (mean 19.0 percent).

Turnout did fall sharply following projections, but in each comparison it fell even more in the elections without projections. This pattern is not an artificial product of "occasional" voters venturing out in the morning only for competitive (unprojected) elections. The years under study had considerable variation in absolute levels of turnout for

Table 7.2   Los Angeles County 7:00–8:00 P.M. Turnout as a Percentage of All Votes Cast

Projected		Unprojected	
Election (Projected 6:17–7:30)	Percentage Cast 7:00–8:00	Elections	Percentage Cast 7:00–8:00
1988	9.01	1976	7.11
		2000	7.95
		2004	7.54
Mean	9.01	Mean	7.53

both projected and unprojected elections—whether calculated as a percentage of the estimated voting-age or voting-eligible population. And the unprojected baseline years spanned both the high side (2004) and the bottom (2000) of that turnout range.

Off-Year Elections

The Los Angeles County records can be exploited for an additional comparison, this one based on eight off-year general elections. In these years, Californians "only" elect their governor and other state and local offices, representative for the U.S. House, and perhaps one of their U.S. senators. Statewide turnout in off-years has been roughly one-fifth to one-third lower than in presidential elections.

Hourly turnout patterns are fairly similar for all eight off-year elections from 1974 through 2002. The standard deviation each hour does not exceed ±1.3 percent, except the first hour in the morning (±1.7 percent). For off-year elections, early morning participation is not as heavy as it is in presidential elections, and late hours are relatively more important. The day culminates with one-third of the votes cast in the last three hours after many people get off work, always peaking between 5:00 and 7:00 P.M. and declining steeply in the final hour (see Figure 7.3).

Perhaps off-year elections prompt less worry about long lines after work. Whatever the reasons for the distinct flow, off-year elections had proportionately fewer votes cast after 6:00 P.M. than was the case during presidential elections of either type. Late-day turnout in off-year elections seems to be such a different phenomenon that it makes a poor basis for comparison with late-day turnout in any presidential election.[4]

Summary

Broad and consistent patterns were seen in hourly voter turnout records of representative Los Angeles County precincts for sixteen elections over thirty years. Examining late-day turnout as a percentage of total turnout, postprojection turnout was slightly higher in every instance than turnout during the corresponding period of the unprojected elections. Turnout did decrease following projections—but it decreased even more during the same time period in years without projections.

Figure 7.3   Los Angeles County Turnout in Off-Year, Projected, and Unprojected Elections

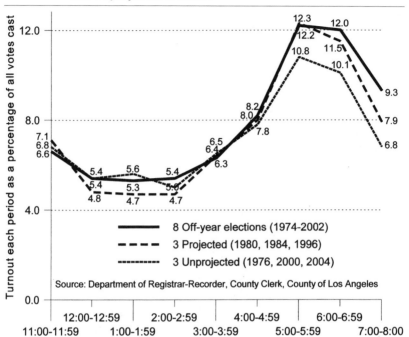

Notes

1. The mean turnout difference in these selected precincts and countywide was less than 1.6 percent. The Office of the Registrar Recorder has tracked hourly turnout primarily to answer journalists' questions about turnout during the course of election day.

2. For 2004, the percentages reported in this chapter are based on the precincts without gaps in their afternoon record-keeping (eleven precincts where 6,391 people voted).

3. Two hours in the 1976 data are problematic. Only 0.9 percent of the votes were shown as cast during the noon hour. While midday is slow at Los Angeles polls, the mean for all presidential years for that hour was 5.2 percent; the lowest recorded for any other noon hour was 4.2 percent. The second oddity was that 1976 is the sole case among sixteen general elections with turnout recorded as increasing in the final hour; other elections usually showed a sharp decline. These two strange entries, Percy Tannenbaum and Leslie Kostrich

(1983, p. 70) determined, were "an apparent recording error." They concluded: "[V]otes cast between noon and 1 p.m. were not properly recorded and they seem to have been included in the critical post-7 p.m. figure, making it suspiciously inflated." Following Tannenbaum and Kostrich's assessment, the 1976 noon hour was adjusted to the mean noon turnout and that increase was subtracted from the inflated last hour. With or without the amended 1976 figures, turnout patterns in the other unprojected elections yield the same results.

4. See the discussion of the Wolfinger and Linquiti study (1981) in Chapter 2 ("Two Outlier Surveys").

8

Deploring but Ignoring Projections: Washington, Oregon, and California

Can additional lessons be learned by turning to a qualitative approach—specifically, focus groups? Qualitative research typically relies on in-depth, open-ended interviews or observations (instead of highly structured questionnaires) and targets a fairly small number of subjects chosen purposively (not a large random sample). Findings from these small nonrandom groups are usually presented as a narrative essay without statistical analysis. A cautious use of qualitative research is to treat the insights gained as valuable for exploratory purposes and needing confirmation by subsequent studies.

Many quantitative social scientists consider qualitative methods to be a primitive, "touchy-feely" approach that makes it far too easy for analysts to infuse, unintentionally or otherwise, their own preexisting biases into the process. In rebuttal, qualitative researchers say that being less structured allows them to be open to unanticipated issues and perspectives that quantitative researchers omit from inflexible questionnaires. Both arguments have merit. In recent years, battle lines have become less rigid, as more quantitative scholars have come to concede the value of more open-ended, in-depth, exploratory approaches, especially as a component of a larger research effort such as this investigation of projections.

At the outset, qualitative analysts usually acknowledge their own subjective role and become more conspicuous in the text by writing in the first person. In that spirit, I will shift to the first person to recount a series of focus groups in Oregon, Washington, and California.

Embarking on Focus Groups

November 6, 1984, was the first time I had been in the West on election day and it was a distinctly different experience. TV news had a certain surreal quality, as if it were being broadcast through a time warp. As CBS declared Ronald Reagan the winner, it was not yet dark outside. The sun had barely set and it was still twilight. Nearly three hours remained for casting ballots. That evening, listening to Oregonians denounce projections, I became interested in delving deeper into attitudes, not just turnout behavior. Focus groups offered an ideal way to explore those attitudes.

A "focus group" is a discussion session, preferably with ten to twelve people, a size that optimizes participation. The moderator raises questions from a flexible agenda, then loosely facilitates the ensuing conversations, trying to engage the reticent and ensure that all viewpoints are welcomed. The setting is ideal for follow-up questions to probe attitudes in more detail. Focus groups ordinarily last between ninety minutes and two hours. (For more on focus group methods, see Krueger and Casey, 2000; Fern and Fern, 2001; and Morrison, 2003.)

Over a fifteen-year period, I conducted eight focus groups with a total of seventy-four voting-age registered voters residing in California, Oregon, and Washington. Four sessions were in California (n = 41 participants)—two in Los Angeles (1993), one in Orange County (1993), and one in San Diego (1999). Two sessions (n = 20) were held in Seattle, Washington (1997). Portland, Oregon (1984), was the site of the two initial impromptu smaller sessions (n = 13).

Although these eight groups were conducted over a fifteen-year period in three different states, the opinions voiced in the discussions were remarkably consistent. That extraordinary consistency adds weight to the findings and justifies reporting the results together.

In recruiting people for the focus groups, the sole screening criterion was that an individual be registered to vote. Participants were predominantly middle-class citizens in their thirties, forties, and fifties, most of whom were regular voters who were at least mildly interested in politics. Just four had retired and only three were under twenty-five. They represented a broad spectrum from lower middle class to upper middle class, with only three who might be counted as poor and none rich. Overall, they were somewhat better educated than the public at large and almost half were college graduates. The groups included Hispanic Americans, African Americans, and Asian Americans, while the majority (fifty-five) were non-Hispanic whites. The gender mix was close (two more women than men). While small groups like these are not statistically precise microcosms, these formed a reasonable congregation whose middle-age, middle-class features were not unlike the registered West Coast electorate.

Agenda

Six central questions (all followed by "why" and "tell me more") were posed whenever they seemed to flow best during the discussions:

1. "What do you think about TV networks projecting the winner before the polls close here?"
2. "Have projections ever kept you from voting?"
3. "Have projections ever kept anyone you know well from voting?"
4. "How do you personally feel on election day when you hear the projections?"
5. "If strong evidence were to show that projections do not discourage people from voting, would that change your attitude?"
6. "Do you believe anything should be done about projections? If so, what?"

In asking these and related questions, my efforts to be a very neutral facilitator surprised some people who assumed that anyone with a minimum level of intelligence (and not working for a TV network) must be openly hostile to projections.

Ire

When the topic of projections was first broached, the usual reaction was indignation: "unfair," "outrageous," "just not right," "makes me mad," "totally irresponsible." In a typical session, one person out of ten would be indifferent and one or two slightly displeased, but seven or eight were usually more bothered by projections. Comments quoted in the rest of this chapter are drawn disproportionately from the majorities, who were more concerned and more outspoken.[1]

A few were perplexed:

> I don't understand how they can do that.

> Why do they allow them to do that?

> Isn't that illegal or unconstitutional or something?

Such questions were always answered by another person who would explain that it was not illegal even though it was "wrong." Someone usually said the networks do it because they are "run by ratings" and desire "to make a buck" no matter what damage is done in the West.

Anecdotes and Hearsay

Trying to push toward more specific critiques, I asked for further explanations of why projections are considered so bad. Answers often turned to horror stories about voters leaving the polls when learning about the network verdicts: "I heard about long lines where people just said 'the heck with it, why should I waste my time if it's all over now,' and that doesn't surprise me one bit." This impact was part of the conventional wisdom that "everybody knows": "Everybody knows that lots of people don't vote after TV says it's finished. They should, but they don't."

Some discussants in Oregon in 1984 recounted secondhand stories about the 1980 election:

> I heard the polls were almost empty the last hour or so in 1980.

> My neighbor who's a big Democrat was mad at her sister-in-law who didn't vote, and she said it was because they'd said Reagan already beat Carter.

A few people escalated the alleged consequences to sweeping changes in election results. One commented: "It's awful that Republicans won lots of seats in Congress because so many Democrats didn't go to the polls after they heard Reagan won." To which a Republican replied, with two others nodding in agreement: "Wait, we don't like it any more than you do."

A vocal antiliberal flavor in the one Orange County session was one of few differences among the eight focus groups. Some participants in that session saw ABC, CBS, and NBC as thoroughly leftist entities that were malevolent on this as well as other issues:

What else would you expect from . . . arrogant New York liberals? Do you think they care for even a second what average people like us think?

They don't try to be fair when they cover conservatives campaigning. . . . Why would they be fair to us out here [in the West] when they cover the results?

Whatever their politics, nearly all participants seemed to believe—as a self-evident indisputable truth—that projections depress voter turnout. Only a handful seemed to lack such crystallized opinions on the subject.

Firsthand Experiences

After listening to anecdotes, I always asked whether participants had ever personally seen anyone walk away from the polls while blaming projections; none ever had. I asked if they had heard firsthand from a credible friend or family member who specifically blamed projections for not voting; none had. I inquired if they personally had ever skipped voting because of projections; none had. I probed as to whether they had ever been seriously tempted to skip voting after hearing projections; none had, although many said they usually had already voted by the time they heard projections.

Despite their reliance on hearsay, their belief that projections damage turnout was so widespread that some participants were stunned that I would pursue it. After a few of my follow-up questions, I was sometimes asked, "Surely you don't think they're harmless, do you?" When I professed uncertainty or neutrality, most seemed astonished but then apparently adjusted to the idea of another eccentric professor missing the obvious point.

Personal Reactions

Participants rarely volunteered any specific personal reasons for disliking projections. I usually had to push to find out more about how projections made them feel personally:

I didn't like it.
[Why didn't you like it?]
It's wrong. It's not right. Uh, it's not fair.
[Why do you feel it isn't right or fair?]

Some people could not initially articulate much more than a vague sense of being wronged. Others eventually expressed one or both of two overlapping sentiments:

1. *Inequality* due to not being treated equally to their fellow citizens living farther east.
2. *Devaluation* because, even if they had already voted, they saw their vote and their state being dismissed as irrelevant.

When the sentiments of inequality and devaluation were voiced, they never once evoked dissent. To the contrary, they resonated with others who said "yes," "exactly," "amen":

Our votes should count just as much as theirs do.

Makes you feel like we don't count.

We're just as much a part of the country as they are.

It's really like a bias against us.

A few of these expressions had a strong populist tone. For example:

They think they run the country anyway and they're just rubbing our noses in it.
[Who are "they"?]
The big shots in New York and Washington.

One aspect of the inequality/unfairness theme was the view that people in the East would never stand for being told the presidency had already been decided while they were still voting. Turning the discussion to a different angle, I asked: "What if it turns out that early TV projections really do *not* keep people in your state from going to the polls? What if researchers can absolutely document that all the people who are going to vote do vote—with or without projections? Would that evidence make you comfortable with projections?" After a short pause to ponder this strange scenario, the answer was always essentially: "No, not really, I still wouldn't like them."

To the follow-up question of why, the issues that were eventually raised were again inequality and devaluation:

> Makes me feel like a second-class citizen.

> I have to tell myself that my vote really will count, regardless of what they say on TV.

Why, I asked, did they not just avoid the news media to keep from being aggravated? Why not just turn off the dial or switch to another channel? Some said that they did this, but that they did not have to watch it themselves to know it was happening:

> Well, I don't look at it 'til later, but it still makes me mad 'cause I know what they were telling everybody.

> I usually don't get off work until, oh, about 6:30 or so but someone always sticks their head in my office and says, "Did you hear . . . ?" That really bugs me.
> [Your coworker or the networks?]
> Both.

In most sessions, as participants warmed to the topic, someone raised the centrality of voting in a democracy:

> They browbeat us all the time on going to vote—and that's OK, they ought to push people to vote—it's super important—but don't turn around and do this [projections] to me.

> Voting is it. It's about the only chance that we've got [gesturing to include the group] to have a say.

> People died so we could do it.

> I'm not rich enough . . . to donate thousands of dollars. . . . My only voice is my vote. That's it.

> You see these poor people in other countries who don't have freedom, who can't vote. But we do, and we oughta put it [voting] up on a pedestal and not do anything, anything to lower, to downgrade it.

Solutions

In three sessions where time allowed, the final question asked was: "What's the solution to the problem that you see here?" A typical first round of answers included:

> They oughta stop.
>
> Just wait a couple of hours, that won't kill anybody.
>
> Just chill 'til it's all over.

After the chorus calling for the networks to "relax" and "just wait a bit," someone would usually say, in a more worldly cynical tone of voice, as did one Californian: "That sounds nice and easy, but I'm telling you, it's not gonna happen. You've gotta have a law to fix it." That idea prompted more head shaking and a few furrowed brows. In three sessions, people issued pleas for voluntary restraint: "I may be a little naive, but why can't they just do the right thing? Why do we have to pass laws all the time to have to force people to do the right thing?" Others said that was "wishful thinking" and "unrealistic." In most groups, at least one person expressed reluctance to "tamper with freedom of the press" by passing a law limiting what journalists could say, comments that seemed to persuade or at least quickly intimidate those who had said "we need a law."

Only one session had time to discuss the idea of a nationwide, uniform poll-closing time. Most withheld judgment but said it sounded good at first glance. Two skeptics assumed that there were probably major problems with it that "we just don't know about yet." A Californian said: "I donno. Sure seems like an awful lot of trouble just 'cause the anchors can't sit still for a couple of hours."

Comparisons with Nationwide Surveys

How representative were the views expressed in these focus groups? They appear to be in step with the general public, at least based on the few available opinion poll questions on the subject. While western opinions may be more intense, nationwide surveys over the years have consistently recorded overwhelming opposition to projections while Americans are still voting.

In 1980, a national poll by the *Los Angeles Times* found that 71 percent believed that "even though they knew who had won the presidential election, the news media should not have announced the results until the polls were closed in all parts of the country." Twenty years later, seven out of ten Americans still shared that view.

The summer 2000 poll by Freedom Forum's First Amendment Center found that 70 percent disagreed (53 percent strongly, 17 percent somewhat) that "television networks should be allowed to project winners of an election while people are still voting." When asked again in 2001, after the calamitous Florida projections, the share who objected jumped to 80 percent and intensified (67 percent objected strongly, 13 percent somewhat).[2]

Nationwide Freedom Forum surveys found that, like participants in the western focus groups, most Americans (64 percent in both 2000 and 2001) believed that projections do discourage people from voting. Indeed, the postelection survey for Pew's Center for the People and the Press even found that 52 percent believed that the networks' mistake of rapidly projecting Gore as the victor in Florida had an "effect on how people in other parts of the country voted."[3]

All the highly antiprojection answers summarized above are nationwide results. To be sure, opinions among Westerners were even stronger in polls as well as in the eight focus groups.

Summary

Eight focus groups with seventy-four registered voters in California, Oregon, and Washington repeatedly produced similar reactions and discussions about election projections. Participants uniformly assumed, based mainly on anecdotes, that projections keep many people from voting. Yet they themselves had never been deterred by projections, nor did they have any personal knowledge of someone who was deterred.

Participants initially "projected" their hostility toward projections onto the damage supposedly done to other people, but ultimately what they seemed to dislike most was the way projections made them feel about themselves and their own vote—a feeling of being treated inequitably as second-class citizens whose votes were publicly devalued. That explains the paradox of western nonvoters appearing less upset about projections than do voters, because it is the voters who care more about voting and who are more offended by the perceived devaluing of their franchise.

Notes

1. Telephone interviewers for the election evening surveys (Chapter 4) noted that voters initiated unsolicited criticisms of projections far more often than did nonvoters. Similarly, in the focus groups, those who cared the most about the political sphere voiced the most displeasure with projections.

2. A CNN/*Time* poll soon after the 2000 election found that 79 percent believed "the media acted irresponsibly" on election night. The one other relevant question in that same poll: "In announcing election results, do you think the media are more interested in getting results out first, or more interested in getting the results right?" Only 10 percent said accuracy was the media's priority, while 87 percent saw instead a race to be first.

A postelection survey for Pew's Center for the People and the Press found that "the press" was judged to have performed more poorly than the candidates whom the press critiques. Respondents were asked, "What grades ["A" through "F"] would you give to each of the following groups for the way they conducted themselves in the campaign?" Only 19–20 percent gave either George W. Bush or Al Gore a "D" or "F" for their campaign conduct; and majorities gave each of them an "A" or a "B." In contrast, 38 percent gave "the press" a failing or near failing grade for "the way they conducted themselves in the campaign." Only 28 percent gave the press an "A" or a "B."

3. Despite 80 percent wanting projections suspended while people vote, the 2001 Freedom Forum survey found the public to be more divided regarding restrictions on media content. When asked about "a law that restricts" the news media from "projecting the winner," 53 percent favored such a law and 45 percent opposed it.

9

Sorting Through
2000 Snafus: Florida

In November 2000, projections became more controversial than ever in U.S. history. Paradoxically, it happened without any projection of the White House winner before the polls closed in all states. The biggest problems centered around the networks awarding Florida prematurely twice, first to Al Gore and then to George W. Bush, when Florida was actually too close to call.

Five of the projection-related controversies of the 2000 election are examined in this chapter, ignoring the many other Florida disputes such as butterfly ballots, dimpled chads, and various lawsuits. The chronology in Table 9.1 reviews the timing of some of those Florida-related events using EST, the major time zone in Florida.[1]

Impact of Unjustified Bush Projection

> Claim 1: The early-morning projection of a Bush victory prompted
> Gore's concession and gave Bush an undeserved psychological
> victory that ultimately put him in the White House.

For the first time in U.S. history, projections made *after* all the polls closed were alleged to have influenced the outcome of the election. Projections spurred Al Gore's telephoned concession and their retraction put the vice president in the awkward position of withdrawing his concession. Some Democrats believe that the early-morning anointment of Bush conferred a presumption of legitimacy on the Texas gov-

Table 9.1 Florida-Related Chronology

EST P.M.	*Tuesday, November 7, 2000*
7:00	Polls closed in Florida's eastern time zone.
7:00–8:00	Newscasters repeatedly announced that Florida's polls were closed while they were still open in nine CST counties.
7:49–8:02	Gore awarded Florida (7:49 NBC, 7:50 CBS, 8:02 ABC).
8:00	Polls closed in Florida's nine CST counties.
9:00	Gore portrayed as a strong favorite after Pennsylvania joins Michigan and Florida in the Gore column.
9:54–10:15	Networks retract the Florida call for Gore.
EST A.M.	*Wednesday, November 8, 2000*
2:17–2:20	Bush awarded Florida and declared the next president.
2:30	Gore concedes to Bush.
3:30	Gore calls Bush to withdraw his concession.
3:50	Networks begin retractions of the second Florida call.

ernor that remained with him even after the networks rescinded their calls.[2]

This speculation, provocative as it is, cannot be empirically tested and will be left for commentators to debate. Gore's brief admission of losing may well have provided the Bush forces with an initial lift and a bumper-sticker slogan, although it seems doubtful that this slim advantage ultimately mattered much once lawyers and judges took over. It remains a matter of supreme irony, after decades of controversy over the impact of projections aired hours before the polls close, that projections broadcast hours after voting ended (and when few people were awake) also would be alleged to have influenced an election's outcome.

Impact of Unjustified Gore Momentum

Claim 2: Having precipitously awarded Florida to Gore early in the evening, the networks depicted Gore on the road to victory for two crucial hours, depressing the turnout of Republican-leaning voters.

After he was credited with Florida, Gore was indeed the beneficiary of encouraging coverage. At 9:00 P.M., when Pennsylvania joined Florida and Michigan in Gore's column, Gore had then won the crucial "trifecta" (CNN's Bob Novak), the "big three" (ABC's Peter Jennings), the "iron triangle" (Fox's Brit Hume). Gore's standing soared among the assembled pundits.

Some Republicans believed this coverage was tantamount to handing the crown to Gore, and sometimes it did veer close to doing just that. Not every commentator jumped on the bandwagon, but many did. With an occasional caveat, Gore was said to be so strong that Bush's only chance would be if he could make a "clean sweep" (Tim Russert on NBC) and "run the table" (Fred Barnes on Fox and Jeff Greenfield on CNN, among others) to carry all remaining contested states.

Some critics believed these quasi-projections were devastating to Bush and even cost him the popular vote majority. Assuming that many demoralized Republicans would not vote, Bill Sammon wrote: "If the networks had refrained from calling states early—or at least called them accurately—Bush might have netted hundreds of thousands of additional votes. . . . [I]f not for the networks' early and erroneous projections, Bush might easily have won the popular vote and carried a few congressional seats with him" (2001, p. 55).

After the Florida call was eventually retracted, the race was portrayed as neck-and-neck, as it should have been all along, but some critics like Sammon believed serious harm had already been done. Did Gore's (temporary) momentum among chatting TV commentators reduce the turnout of Republican voters?

Even with unequivocal projections, the research reported in previous chapters uncovered little or no evidence of decreased turnout. So it seems far-fetched that many prospective Bush voters would have been deterred by the mere likelihood that a projection might be issued for Gore at a later point. However, some angry Republicans firmly believed that nearly two hours of misleading, prime-time, rosy scenarios for Gore must have added injury to insult.

Hourly data of voter turnout in Los Angeles County (the basis of Chapter 7) can provide an empirical test. The county included many GOP voters (Bush received 871,930 votes), although they were highly outnumbered (Gore received 1,710,505 votes). Among the thirty precincts where hourly turnout was tracked, two precincts where Bush garnered nearly 60 percent of the vote stood out as more Republican. In locales like these, relative late-day turnout should have been depressed if fragile Bush sympathizers were truly demoralized by Gore's apparent advances.

Figure 9.1 (calculating hourly turnout as a percentage of all votes cast) shows that turnout was relatively lower during most of the after-

Figure 9.1   Los Angeles County Turnout in Republican Precincts vs. Countywide

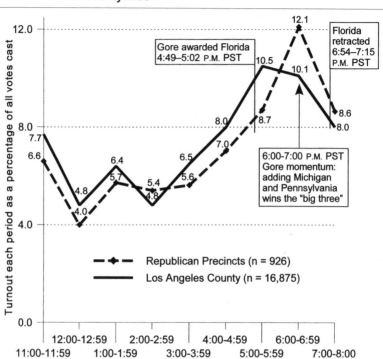

noon in the more Republican precincts, where proportionately more people had voted in the morning. After Florida was assigned to Gore, the increased turnout in the 5:00 hour over the 4:00 hour was proportionately about the same in the GOP and countywide samples. However, during the hour of Gore's greatest momentum, when he was reported to have swept the "big three" pivotal states, relative turnout surged in the more Republican neighborhoods. Far from being scared away from the polls, turnout increased 38 percent (8.8 to 12.2 percent) over the previous hour in the Republican precincts. At the same time, turnout countywide slowed (from 10.5 to 10.1 percent).[3]

Conceivably, the 6:00–7:00 surge could have been disproportionately composed of galvanized Democrats in those Republican-leaning precincts. If so, that should also be reflected to an even greater degree in the countywide total, which was even more Democratic, and that was not the case. Overall, the Los Angeles County data show no hint that the impending threat of a Gore victory frightened Republicans away from the polls.

Impact of Unjustified Gore Call on the Panhandle

Claim 3: Calling Florida for Gore before the polls closed in the CST panhandle of Florida depressed turnout in that Republican-leaning region, causing a net loss to Bush of thousands of votes.

In fact, the networks did not begin announcing that Gore had won Florida until the doors were about to close at polling stations in the western part of the state: CNN was just five minutes before the deadline, Fox eight, CBS ten, and NBC ten and a half minutes.[4] Were many nonvoters watching television at this late hour but genuinely intending to sprint to the polls (until they heard Gore won Florida)?

A survey by John McLaughlin and Associates, a Republican consulting firm, has been cited as proof that last-minute Florida projections deterred thousands of likely Bush voters. Unfortunately, that survey had leading questions, was conducted after ten contaminating days of postelection press coverage of projection controversies, and claimed that a wildly implausible share of nonvoters (55 percent) heard projections during the ten-minute window and said they were thus "influenced" not to vote (28 percent of the exposed Floridians).[5]

If the McLaughlin numbers are correct, it means that projecting Florida for Gore depressed total voter turnout in the CST panhandle by over 5 percent in about ten minutes. On a per-minute basis, that impact is over 400 times more powerful than was found on election night in Portland, when only about 0.2 percent of all registered voters blamed projections for not voting after three full hours of news diffusion.[6] Could there have been so many ambivalent Floridians (none of them Lance Armstrong or Jeff Gordon) who were honestly considering racing to the polls just as the lights were about to be turned off?[7]

Impact of False News About Closed Florida Polls

Claim 4: For one full hour, the networks repeatedly spread the falsehood that voting had ended in Florida, telling potential voters in the CST panhandle to stay home and thus depressing turnout.

Independent of the flimsy issue of the last-minute projections before panhandle polls closed, this is a more troublesome charge. Over the period of one hour, the networks did misinform viewers about the possibility of voting in Florida. While not a projection, this fiction was usually repeated as part of updating Florida's projection status.

From 6:00 to 7:00 P.M. CST (7 to 8:00 EST), polls were open in the nine westernmost counties of the Florida panhandle that were vital to any chances Bush had to carry Florida in 2000.[8] During that hour, networks announced erroneously that it was no longer possible to vote in Florida. None of the networks got it right,[9] but none surpassed CBS's Dan Rather in his frequent insistence—fifteen times that hour—that it was too late to vote in the state of Florida. Rather said, for example:

> I want to emphasize to you now that the polls are closed in Florida.
>
> I want you to know—keep emphasizing it—Florida, the polls have closed. No decision yet there.

"Keep emphasizing it" Rather did, and his errors were compounded by the map over his shoulder that colored states gray only if the polls were "still open." As he explained several times: "The states in white—these are the states where the polls have closed but where it's too early to make a call—Florida, the big one." Surpassing the population of six states, almost 900,000 people lived in the nine counties in the CST Florida panhandle where the polls were, contrary to network anchors, still open. These counties constituted 6 percent of the total population of the country's fourth-most populous state—where a few hundred votes statewide ultimately decided the presidency.[10]

What was the impact of misinforming over half a million (Republican-leaning) registered voters in western Florida that their polls were closed? To try to answer this formidable question, several approaches can be considered. Sadly, most are forced to rely on measuring turnout as a percentage of the names on unevenly inflated voter registration lists.

The crudest approach is to compare turnout of registered voters in all of EST Florida (70.3 percent) and all of CST Florida (67.0 percent). Of course, this hardly establishes that the networks lowered turnout by 3.3 percentage points in the panhandle. Many other demographic and political factors could account for that gap.

An improvement is to compare changes in CST and EST turnout between 1996 and 2000.[11] Indeed, turnout as a percentage of registered voters increased nearly 3 percentage points in *both* regions, with the gain just 0.03 percent less in the misled CST panhandle. Yet many things changed between the 1996 and 2000 elections,[12] notably the Democratic ticket's onslaught of central and south Florida with a steady stream of visits by Joseph Lieberman, the vice presidential candidate,[13] a strategy expected to push turnout up in the peninsula rather than in the comparatively ignored panhandle.

A third approach is to compare the turnout of matched counties. One researcher compared the nine CST counties with eight EST counties matched for similar voting patterns and similar demographics (Pierce, 2001) and found a turnout gain in the CST panhandle that was 1.5 percentage points *greater* than in the matched EST counties. Another matching study found the 1996–2000 turnout increases to have been almost identical, with a fractionally higher increase (0.3 percentage points) in the EST counties.[14]

A fourth approach is to run multiple-regression equations predicting countywide turnout (again using registration lists) for Florida's sixty counties. Using slightly different sets of control variables, one study (Lott, 2000) found that time zone statistically predicted variation in county turnout,[15] while another multiple-regression study did not (Sobel and Lawson, 2001).[16]

A fifth approach is to consider personal impressions. In a lawsuit, notarized affidavits were presented from over three dozen election officials from the panhandle (Perrin, 2001).[17] All expressed surprise at the sharp decline in turnout they witnessed during the final hour. The Florida testimony echoed observations on the West Coast when the last-hour drop was attributed to projections, although that pattern was common with or without projections (see Chapters 5 and 7).

A sixth approach would have entailed studying late-day voting patterns, but only one actual record of hourly turnout could be located. In a large precinct near the western end of Florida, balloting underwent the sort of final-hour decline that was found to be typical on the West Coast (with or without projections).[18] In that light, the decline recorded at this solitary precinct did not appear unusual, but there was no comparative Florida data from other years or other counties.

Overall, it seems fair to conclude that panhandle voting did not fall sharply in the wake of false information from the networks. Had damage been as severe as some critics claimed, plummeting turnout should have been detectable even with these less-than-ideal data analyses. While a pronounced turnout decline was not measured in the panhandle, it must still be acknowledged that even a small impact (a few hundred rather than tens of thousands), unobservable with available data, would still have mattered greatly with so few votes separating Bush and Gore in the fight over Florida.[19]

What might account for the lack of a strong impact? First, panhandle residents may have learned over the years that the networks often get such facts wrong. Second, anyone who does not already know when local polls close has weeks to learn this information from local newspapers, radio, and local TV news, along with family, friends, neighbors, and coworkers. Third, the hour of error began at 6:00 P.M. CST, when affiliates in Panama City and Mobile–Pensacola–Ft. Walton Beach cut from network news to air half-hour *local* newscasts.[20] With a smaller network window, viewers would not be as likely to hear of "closed" Florida polls.

After the blunders of 2000, fast forward to the off-year election night of 2002 to hear CNN's Jeff Greenfield: "We used to say we will project when the great preponderance of polls in a state have closed. After Florida's last [election] where the panhandle closed late, we will call races only when *all* the polls have closed. . . . I think that's a good thing." Indeed, in 2002 and 2004, anchors on all networks waited until panhandle polls closed before announcing that polls in Florida had closed. Other dual-zone states also received the same restraint.

Impact of "Delayed" Projections

> *Claim 5: Equally competitive states were called much faster when given to Gore than to Bush; commentators inferred from slow calls that Bush was in trouble in his core states, adding to the illusion of Gore momentum and demoralizing would-be Republican voters.*

The first part of this claim is accurate. Excluding landslide states (where the winner's margin was over 15.0 percent and victory was called immediately) and the six cliffhanger states (with margins of less than 1.5 percent),[21] the twenty-two intermediate battleground states were called much more rapidly if they went for Gore.

Figure 9.2 displays the winner's margin plotted by the time elapsed until the median projection was broadcast. Among states where the winning margin was 8 percent to 14 percent, all four Gore states were called instantly by all networks—unlike the four Bush states, which took a

Figure 9.2   Margin of Victory by Time Elapsed Before Median Projection Broadcast by State

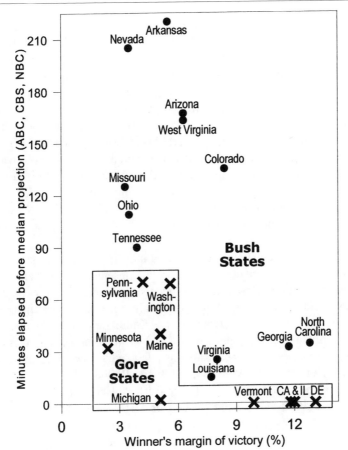

while. For example, thirty-four minutes passed before NBC called North Carolina for Bush (forty-five minutes for ABC, twenty-eight minutes for CBS). During that wait, Tom Brokaw commented: "The idea that North Carolina is still too close to call does come as a surprise this evening." It was surprising, but for the opposite reason: North Carolina ought never have been depicted as "still too close to call." Bush won the state, as expected, with a healthy margin of 13 percent.

Among states won by margins of 2 to 7 percent, no matter how Gore's five and Bush's seven states are compared, the gaps are striking.

Using the ABC, CBS, and NBC median times, *all* five Gore states were typically called within seventy minutes, while *none* of the seven Bush states were called in less than ninety minutes.

Critics were incensed by the long lag in calling Ohio for Bush when Michigan had been called for Gore almost immediately. NBC's Tim Russert saw Ohio as more trouble for Bush: "The fact we projected Florida and Michigan [for Gore] before we projected Ohio for Bush is very telling." In subsequent congressional hearings, network representatives pledged to stop interpreting lags in projections as indicating tight races, since the delays could be due to inadequate and poor data. Responding to angry charges of liberal bias from Representative Billy Tauzin (R–La.), they blamed delays entirely on the Voter News Service (VNS), the consortium created and funded by five networks and the Associated Press to conduct exit polls and count vote totals. Network analysts, they said, were doing the best they could with the VNS data they were given and were not holding back on projecting states for Bush.

The VNS was apparently plagued by inadequate staffing, poor estimation models, unexpected increases in absentee voting, and increased refusal rates. Republicans—increasingly hostile to news media seen as agents of the Democrats—especially refused to participate in exit polls, producing an overcount of the Democratic vote. This was a known problem, but one that increased in 2000 in certain states and that preelection computer models had not adequately taken into account (see also Konner, 2003; Mitofsky, 2003; and Biemer et al., 2003).

For unknown reasons, several solid Bush states had small VNS exit-poll samples. CBS explained its delay for Alabama as due to "a particularly small exit-poll sample of just 20 precincts." Exit-poll results for North Carolina and Georgia were said to lack "enough statistical certainty to make the call at poll closing" (Mason, Frankovic, and Jamieson, 2001, p. 36). An interesting twist supporting the conclusion that VNS, the data-supplier, was the culprit and not the network decision desks, is that Fox News (seldom accused of liberal bias) took *longer* than did ABC, CBS, or NBC to call seven of the thirteen Bush states.[22]

In any event, critics were correct about timing. Contested states that Gore won by 2–15 percent were projected much faster than equally contested states that Bush won. Yet there was no sign that those delays, annoying as they may have been to Republicans, caused any harm. No evidence could be found that potential Republican voters in the West stayed home because Bush was not quickly awarded states like Ohio and North Carolina. As observed earlier, during the peak of Gore's drive, Republican-leaning precincts in Los Angeles County were busier than either before or after Gore seemed to have had so much momentum. So, "delays in projecting Bush states" can be added to the unfortunate series of VNS and network snafus that did not do any observable damage—except perhaps to the credibility of the networks.

Summary

Network coverage of the 2000 election finale was blemished by a series of well-known and not-so-well-known errors. Both Democratic and Republican partisans came away with grievances. And yet, despite misinforming viewers on several noteworthy matters during that evening and the next morning, no evidence could be found of any measurable damage "on the ground" to voter turnout or the election process.

Unjustified award of Florida to Bush the next morning? Yes, but (probably) no ultimate impact. Bush may have gained a momentary psychological advantage from Gore's projection-induced concession, but soon lawyers and courts took over.

Unjustified award of Florida to Gore fueling his TV momentum? Yes, but no sign that it frightened away western Republicans. Gore fans may have relished the two hours of TV glory after their man was awarded Florida, but the best evidence is that westerners were not deterred by Gore's presumed progress any more than by actual projections in years past.

Unjustified award of Florida to Gore while polls were open in the Republican-leaning Florida panhandle? Yes, but doors were practically closing with less than eleven minutes to go. Republicans probably ought to have been angrier about the risks from the following issue.

False statements about all Florida polls being closed while voting was still under way in the panhandle? Yes, but no manifest harm to panhandle turnout, although a nontrivial tiny impact cannot be ruled out.

Delays in calling states for Bush and misinterpretations of those VNS-caused delays? Yes, but alleged momentum does not seem to depress turnout any more than explicit projections do. Besides, the people who really care how long it takes to call Ohio and North Carolina may be the least likely to be dissuaded from voting.

Notes

1. Most election night (and next morning) times are those cited by Alicia Shepard (2001), supplemented by numerous other sources that sometimes differed by one or two minutes regarding some events. For a thoughtful critique of the networks' style and substance in covering election nights in 1968 and 2000, see Patterson, 2003.

2. For example, Bob Schrum said, "It made a big difference that Dan Rather said, 'Let's give a big hearty Texas welcome to the new President of the United States, George W. Bush.'" Schrum and others were quoted in Jamieson and Waldman, 2002, an assessment of framing choices in discourse on Sunday TV talk shows regarding postelection struggles. To Schrum's claim, Republicans replied that the mistake in Bush's favor merely offset all the network errors that favored Gore the night before. In an early-morning apology on NBC, Tom Brokaw said wryly: "We awarded Florida erroneously at one point, came back and managed to make everything equal by awarding it erroneously a second time." Of course, that second mistake did not necessarily even the score if the fumble that aided Bush was ultimately more momentous.

3. The sharp decline typical of the 7:00–8:00 hour came when Florida was retracted and Bush regained a more equal footing. As shown in Figure 9.1, this news did not boost comparative turnout in the Republican precincts any more than Gore's apparent momentum had suppressed it.

4. All the projections were announced suddenly without any advance hints that Florida was leaning to Gore. ABC did not project Florida until two minutes after the polls closed, delayed by having briefly considered and rejected the concerns of some wise analysts who correctly feared the projection was premature.

5. John McLaughlin and Associates conducted a survey of over 600 people who said they were registered to vote in the central time Florida panhandle. An unknown number of nonvoters were weighted up to equal 210 people. Surprisingly, over half of them (55 percent) claimed to have heard a projection during the eleven-minute window. Could the amazing diffusion of projection news among these Florida nonvoters somehow have surpassed in a few minutes what it took three hours to achieve in Portland, as reviewed in Chapter 4? A remarkably large portion (28 percent) of those who claimed they heard the projection said yes to the leading question: "Did the news reports about Al Gore winning Florida influence you not to vote for president?" Suggesting projections as an excuse reinforced any contamination from the high-profile controversy about the topic during the week following the election. Also, the vague word "influence" is not the same as being a decisive reason for nonvoting.

6. Using the 0.22 percent midpoint estimate for total decline in voter turnout in the Portland area; see Chapter 4.

7. Or were thousands of nonvoters in their cars racing for the polling stations to vote at the last minute and politically engaged enough to listen to election news on the radio but still politically disengaged enough to make a U-turn

upon hearing Gore's alleged Florida victory? Using the behavioral findings from Chapters 5, 6, and 7, it is more likely that Bush did not suffer a net loss of any votes.

8. A Florida statute requires that the county seat's time zone be used for uniform poll closings through the county. Since Port St. Joe is in the eastern time zone, polls are closed throughout Gulf County at 7:00 P.M. EST. Gulf is sometimes erroneously grouped with the CST panhandle counties, but its polls are aligned with EST Florida.

9. Nationwide, between 7:00 and 8:00 P.M. EST, CBS broadcast this mistake fifteen times, ABC twice, NBC twice, CNN once, and Fox once. In the previous hour, CNN had twice made erroneous references to Florida polls closing, as did Fox News three times.

10. Florida was not alone. Other dual-zone states were also given short shrift. When Texas, for example, was said to have closed its polls, voting continued for another hour in the western MST tip, which includes the 700,000 residents of El Paso.

11. Along these analytical lines, Bob Beckel, a leading Democratic strategist, directed a study that estimated that there was a turnout decline in the last hour that cost Bush 8,000 votes. That study has not been publicly available, although Beckel explained that it compared changes in the 2000 CST-EST turnout to that of past elections. Personal conversation, June 6, 2003.

12. One can hardly assume that the relative standing of two regions evolved over four years in the same direction at the exact same speed in terms of the population composition, the appeal of the candidates and the issues, the level of inflation in voter registration lists, the magnitude of voter mobilization efforts, and so forth.

13. During the final week, at least one member of the Democratic ticket was in Florida during six of those days, right up to the morning of election day, when Al Gore was still soliciting votes in Tampa. Only twice that week did George Bush or Dick Cheney visit Florida. That fall, Lieberman and Gore spent twice as many days in Florida as did Cheney and Bush. For months, Joe Lieberman had been devoting an extraordinary amount of time to central and south Florida—perhaps a modern U.S. record for one candidate concentrating on one area. From mid-October until election day, Lieberman spent one out of every three days in Florida. The only visit by a major party candidate to Florida's panhandle in the fall was when Cheney stopped by Pensacola in September.

14. Calhoun and Jackson (CST) versus Franklin and Liberty Counties (EST). The demographic match was close in most but not all respects and all four counties were in the same television market (Panama City). This comparison was conducted by the author.

15. Lott's equations showed a strange enormous loss of 7,500 to 37,500 nonvoters confined to the panhandle's Republicans (a group not previously known to be uniquely obedient to network newscasts). Since 2000 census figures had yet to be published, Lott had to use 1998 county estimates for much of his data.

16. Sobel and Lawson ran a multiple-regression equation with time zone and five demographic variables competing to predict change in turnout (1996–2000) in Florida's sixty counties. They concluded there was "no significant impact" on turnout overall or for Bush or Gore.

17. The lawsuit was *Jacob Knight et al. v. Voter News Service et al.* The Voter News Service and the networks were sued for "interfering with the electoral process," violating a Florida statute that makes it a felony to "deceive or deter any elector in voting." This comment from a precinct in Bay County was typical: "Voting was steady all day until 6:00 pm. Between 6:00–7:00 pm, it was very different from past elections. It was empty."

18. Warren Brown, an election official in a large upscale precinct in Santa Rosa County, kept hourly turnout records. Out of 2,674 votes cast, Brown's figures show that turnout fell from 9.0 percent during the 5:00–6:00 period to 5.4 percent during the final 6:00–7:00 hour. That decline is in the range of the final-hour decline often found on the West Coast (see Chapters 5 and 7). However, since Florida voting concludes at 7:00, not 8:00 as in West Coast states, perhaps the final hour in Florida should not undergo such a large decline. Without any other late-day Florida comparisons, the Santa Rosa pattern by itself is inadequate for drawing any inferences.

19. Conceivably, a few newcomers to Florida might have walked past the TV set at 6:40 intending to go vote, heard voting had ended, did not yet have local friends to confer with, and stayed home. Even if such individuals were so undetectably rare that they were only 1 out of every 2,000 voters, they still would have added up to 200–300 lost panhandle votes, numbers that were "big" when counting the Florida returns in 2000.

20. In these two markets that cover the panhandle, network affiliates ran one half-hour local newscast from 5:00 to 5:30 P.M. CST, followed by the flagship network evening news, 5:30–6:00. From 6:00 to 6:30, affiliates returned with another half-hour local newscast.

21. Four of these states were not called until more than three hours had elapsed. The two exceptions, both called for Gore, were Florida (retracted) and New Mexico. The premature New Mexico call turned out to be correct, but a week after the election Bush had a four vote lead until "the discovery of at least 500 more ballots for Gore in southern Dona Ana County put the Democrat ahead by about 375 votes" (CNN, November 14, 2000).

22. Of the four networks, Fox was the *last* to award Bush seven (Alabama, North Carolina, Georgia, Colorado, Louisiana, Arkansas, Tennessee) of these thirteen states. West Virginia was the only Bush state that Fox called significantly earlier than did the big three networks. So, if the big three were delaying Bush calls, Fox usually delayed them even longer. As for giving states to Gore, Fox was last for three (Minnesota, Michigan, Washington) of these nine Gore states; Fox awarded Maine to Gore twenty minutes before any other network and Pennsylvania to Gore twenty minutes before ABC and ten minutes before NBC.

10

Equity, Fairness, and Policy Options

In 1916 the *Oregon Journal,* Portland's afternoon newspaper, featured the election day banner headline: HUGHES ELECTED. Its 2:00 P.M. edition lead was based on reports that Charles Everett Hughes was sweeping the East. History soon recorded Woodrow Wilson as the true winner. Critics alleged that the newspaper's headline discouraged people from voting. One claimed: "Thousands did not vote at all."[1]

Just over half a century later, television networks became the founts of election projections and made grand strides in accuracy, rarely making mistakes, although the Florida fiascos of 2000 and misleading leaks of 2004 scarred their reputation. Projecting the next president early—over 100 minutes before polls closed on the West Coast in seven of the twelve elections, 1960 through 2004—became a staple of broadcast coverage (see Table 1.1).

While now routine, projections are no less controversial, and large majorities of Americans tell pollsters that the networks should wait before declaring the end to the presidential race. Perhaps more public and political pressure is not generated because the controversy, while recurrent, erupts no more than once every four years, then attention shifts as more pressing issues recapture the public agenda. Antiprojection forces have also lacked clear and convincing evidence that projections really do keep many people from voting.

Whether or not projections do deter "thousands" from voting, as the critic in 1916 and many others thereafter have charged, has been the key question addressed in this book. Do projections decrease voter turnout? The findings, based on multiple methods, varied sites, and many elections, may be summarized as follows:

- In a large election night survey in the Portland area, few nonvoters blamed projections and they constituted only a fraction of all valid registered voters (0.2 percent). A majority of nonvoters never heard any projection news before polls closed.
- Hourly voter turnout in two closely matched, adjacent Oregon counties in two different time zones showed no sign that late-day turnout was depressed at all in the county exposed to the additional hour of projections.
- Matched counties on either side of time zones in Idaho, Kansas, and North Dakota all failed to show lower turnout of registered voters in counties more exposed to projections.
- Time-series comparisons of decades of hourly voter turnout in Los Angeles County did not reveal a single instance of postprojection turnout being lower than the turnout for comparable late-day periods in close, unprojected presidential elections.
- Eight focus groups with registered voters in Oregon, Washington, and California uncovered no firsthand knowledge of people abstaining because of projections; however, these westerners still disliked projections as inequitable and demeaning.
- Various network errors related to projections in the 2000 election did not produce any detectable decrease in voter turnout either in the Florida panhandle or in Los Angeles.

Consistent with these findings, the vast literature on voter turnout indicates that by the time election day arrives, citizens already have many complex, lifelong personal and structural influences on their decision to vote or not to vote. Those propensities are not easily transformed by happening to hear projection news.

A curious divergence emerged in the findings that, while not large, is worth noting. The election night survey in Chapter 4 found a few nonvoters who blamed projections, roughly one-fifth of 1 percent of valid registered voters. In contrast, none of the other methodologies found any net turnout decline linked to projections. What might explain this small discrepancy? One possibility is that most nonvoters who blamed projections used it (consciously or unconsciously) as a convenient excuse for failing to do their "civic duty." If so, the survey estimate of projection effects, while quite small, is still an exaggeration. A second possibility is that, for a few people, projections stimulate turnout, perhaps by adding an urgency to the last chance to put their opinions on the record. If so, they might offset the tiny group who say they are discouraged by projection news. This could explain why, in the findings reported in Chapters 5 through 7, greater exposures to projections were so consistently linked to very slightly *higher* levels of voter turnout.

In light of the findings from prior chapters, should any public policies be changed because of projections? The classic steps in policy analysis are to define the problem, assemble evidence, construct alternatives, select evaluation criteria, and estimate the outcomes and trade-offs of alternative policies.[2]

Define the Problem and Assemble Evidence

As noted in Chapter 1, critics primarily defined the problem as "network projections decreasing voter turnout." This claim, however plausible it sounded, has not been substantiated. Faced with a strong body of evidence to the contrary, this particular argument against projections has collapsed. The turnout criterion meant that any policy change would have to be justified by western voters being more derelict and less conscientious (i.e., more vulnerable to projections). By this standard, their resilience in voting during the hours after projections means that projections do no harm.

If depressed turnout is the only issue to be addressed, the debate is over and there is no need to contemplate changes in public policy. Lowered turnout, however, is not the sole issue. An alternative problem definition can be considered, one that has become lost in all the attention given the more tangible idea of decreased turnout. Ignoring turnout, this problem definition focuses entirely on fairness and equity. This argument against projections is not that they influence the westerners who do not vote; it is that they demean the westerners who do vote.

Not everyone will agree that strengthening fairness and respect—in the absence of any demonstrable harm beyond "hurt feelings"—is sufficient to merit shifts in public policy. Indeed, this particular problem definition may not raise the stakes to a level that would justify drastic changes in public policy and any major new expenditure of taxpayer dollars. Nevertheless, having just rejected the turnout claim, consider the merits of this alternative way of framing the issue.

Voting is more than a mundane cyclical activity, more than a mere ritual of democracy; it is the heart of the democratic republican form of government. While political power is wielded in many ways by money and pressure groups—and media conglomerates—voting remains the chief way for average Americans to try to influence the direction of public policy. A national election is a remarkable event—no riots, no guns, no coups d'etat—just tens of millions of diverse citizens, spread over thousands of miles, peacefully picking their representatives. Isn't it essential to protect the sanctity of the process from anything, not just fraud or poor voting machines, that might damage its integrity? Why would responsible people want to do anything that would diminish this elemental act in the slightest?

Asserting that "the consent of the governed" ought to be exalted, not devalued, is of course a value-laden argument. But if these are values worth supporting, it is because they are rooted in treating fellow citizens equitably and honorably. In overwhelming numbers in surveys and focus groups, westerners communicate their resentment at being publicly discounted when told repeatedly that the presidency has been decided without the input of their votes. Perhaps they should feel lucky to be benevolently told that "there are still a lot of local races left to decide," but that does not seem to be much consolation for their perceived second-class citizenship.

To be sure, regional equality does not strike as deep a chord as does the issue of racial equality, a matter of justifiable American sensitivity. Perhaps California's prominence as the most populated state and one that is predominantly Hispanic, Asian, and African American will put pressure on journalists to be more inclusive when presenting the nation's election decisions.

All told, the problem of projections is not that broadcasters are driving away many thousands of would-be voters; it is a more subtle issue of equity and respecting the shared role of fellow citizens. If this argument is persuasive, are there any appropriately tailored policy responses to all those westerners who believe that their votes are denigrated by election day projections?

Construct Alternatives and Select Evaluation Criteria

Many proposals have been offered for dealing with projections. Percy Tannenbaum and Leslie Kostrich (1983) devoted 130 pages of their book to a detailed analysis of the pros and cons of over a dozen options. Decades later these ideas are still the main options on the policy table, and little has changed regarding their advantages and disadvantages. Table 10.1 lists the major proposals without all their numerous variations.

Tannenbaum and Kostrich evaluated these options with well-chosen criteria that can be organized as follows:

- *Legality:* Is the proposal legitimate under the Constitution, particularly with respect to free speech?
- *Benefits:* Would the problem be eliminated or mitigated?
- *Costs:* How extensive and expensive are required administrative and other changes? Are there negative side effects?
- *Equity:* Are benefits and costs distributed fairly?

It would be sad if a "reform" itself dampened voter turnout. Since policy shifts sometimes can cause more problems than they solve, a fifth criterion is added here to put an explicit premium on caution:

Table 10.1 Policy Proposals

Limitations on speech and/or data collection
- Prohibit all interviews with voters on election day or near polls
- Require exit polls begin with a discouraging "Miranda warning"
- FCC ban on projecting elections electronically before polls close
- Congressional ban on projections before polls close
- Prohibit states from releasing vote results until, e.g., 11 P.M. EST

Uniform poll closings
- Regular Tuesday voting with modifications
     Later poll closings in the East (e.g., close nationwide at 11 P.M. EST)
     Earlier poll closings in the West (e.g., close nationwide at 9 P.M. EST)
- Special voting days
     Sunday voting (e.g., nationwide noon to 9 P.M. EST)
     Election day holiday (e.g., close nationwide at 8 P.M. EST)
- Monday/Tuesday voting
     Twenty-four-hour voting day (e.g., noon Monday to noon Tuesday EST)
     Modified twenty-four-hour period (ending simultaneously)

Other
- Two-week delay of daylight saving time in the Pacific time zone
- Voluntary restraint by TV networks until more polls close

- *Increments:* Would the changes be modest ones that minimize risks and that could be easily reversed or adjusted?

Likely Outcomes and Tradeoffs

Most proposals assumed that projections were markedly depressing turnout and changing election outcomes in the West. Even for a problem of that magnitude, many of the proposals are quite aggressive. The first five proposals in Table 10.1 are a challenge to the first criteria of legality and free speech, and the next six proposals confront severe problems of cost and uncertain benefits.

The first set of proposals involves limits on who can say what to whom—regulating the communication of exit-poll interviewers or network journalists. All these ideas entail worrisome constitutional issues involving unfortunate infringements on the freedom of speech. While Canada has a law against projections, U.S. law and tradition make free speech a paramount value and there is no compelling reason to consider tinkering with free speech here.

The second series of proposals consists of uniform poll-closing ideas mandating that all states finish voting at the same time nationwide, with some versions exempting Alaska and Hawaii. Many of these systems would be expensive and involve serious administrative headaches, especially the twenty-four-hour proposals. Elections already cost many millions of dollars, and adding even a few hours to an already long schedule may require a second shift, pose staffing difficulties, necessitate more security precautions, and cost disproportionately more money.

Adding another national holiday would be costly as well, imposing productivity costs in both the public and private sectors. Moreover, an election day holiday on a Tuesday would set up a tempting four-day minivacation opportunity with unknown consequences for voter turnout. Sunday voting might not cost more but does prompt strenuous objections from many religious groups—not to be taken lightly in the quest to be more respectful of fellow citizens.

Any version of uniformity that would close all polls nationwide at 9:00 P.M. EST forces West Coast polls to close at 6:00 P.M. PST. Eliminating two hours of postwork voting on the commuter-intensive West Coast would surely discourage voting far more than TV projections ever did. Using 11:00 P.M. EST for the uniform closing would remove the threat to the West Coast (where closings would stay at 8:00 P.M. PST) but pushes all the inconvenience (and unknown effects) to the more heavily populated East Coast, where most morning voting hours would be lost unless a costly second shift were added.

A Modest Proposal

Instead of costly and potentially counterproductive options or attempts to curtail speech, two incremental steps have considerable potential to ameliorate the situation:

1. The new "all polls closed in a state" projection policy.
2. A delay of western daylight saving time.

The first step, it appears, has already been taken. In 2002 and 2004, the networks began waiting until all—not just most—polls closed in a state before calling that state. If this practice continues—some observers have questioned whether the networks will maintain this restraint for long (Mitofsky, 2001)—it effectively will delay the earliest possible projection by one full hour. This reform takes Texas, Michigan, and Kansas out of the large group of states that are projectable by 5:00 P.M. PST, leaving only 269 callable electoral votes—one short of the number needed to win.[3] This one-hour delay pushes back the earliest projection until after the end of the heavy postwork voting hour (5:00–6:00 P.M. PST) on the West Coast.

Thanks to this respectful adjustment by the networks, the value of a second small shift in public policy would be magnified. If West Coast states extend daylight saving time for just two weeks in leap years (or every year), potential exposure to projections would be delayed by another hour. Since daylight saving time now ends the last Sunday in October, it would only need to be extended another two weeks on the West Coast.

The proposal is a reasonable one and is politically feasible. Congress would need to endorse the extension of daylight saving time, but there would be no financial or administrative burden on taxpayers in other parts of the country. Moreover, California has already endorsed the idea of extending DST. During California's 2001 energy crisis, the legislature passed a joint resolution requesting that the state be permitted to use DST all year long.[4] A series of studies had concluded that the energy savings would be substantial[5]—evading one hour of potential projections would be a nice side benefit.

Although Congress and the White House did not act on the request, the idea remains a good one. With sufficient notice, transit schedules and other time-sensitive enterprises should be able to adjust to ending daylight saving time in mid-November (or not ending DST at all under the legislature's plan) as easily as doing so at the end of October. If westerners are serious about removing the affront of projections, this is a simple, money-saving strategy they can pursue immediately.

The combined result of these two modifications—extending DST two weeks on the West Coast and the new "all polls closed" practice—would be to reduce the maximum window of potential West Coast exposure to projections from three hours to one hour. Even that one hour might be rare if the networks are as cautious in issuing projections in the future as they were in 2004.

New circumstances may force network analysts to adopt a slightly slower pace. Reliance on exit polls may become more difficult if refusal rates continue to climb in ways that cannot be precisely estimated in advance and fully accommodated into computer models. The surge in mail-in and absentee balloting adds another level of complexity to building predictive equations and data gathering. Also, the networks will probably want to continue to be extremely careful during the years following their credibility-damaging failures in the 2000 election.

The cumulative consequences should result in slower projections of some states, perhaps five minutes here, thirty minutes there. If so, it will take longer to project the White House winner safely, thereby getting closer to and perhaps beyond final poll closings in Pacific *daylight* time.[6] If in ensuing elections—despite the greatly narrowed window—westerners still find themselves subjected to offensive amounts of projections during 7:00–8:00 P.M. PDT, other options, such as small adjustments to western poll-closing times,[7] might then be considered.

To date, when faced with projections, westerners have deplored but ignored them. They cast ballots even after network anchors have told them, in no uncertain terms, that the most important contest of the day is over. At the same time, westerners still abhor projections as a demeaning and unfair practice that publicly relegates them to "other local races," denying their standing as equal citizens on election day. Due to a small policy shift by the networks, a small policy shift on daylight saving time in Pacific time states should greatly reduce the risk that early projections will be seen as devaluing the still undeterred voters in the West.

Notes

1. Cited in Walter M. Pierce, "Climbing on the Bandwagon," *Public Opinion Quarterly* 4 (June 1940): 241–243.

2. See, for example, Bardach, 2000, for a similar enumeration and discussion of these steps.

3. These numbers are based on the electoral votes allocated for the 2004 and 2008 elections (see Chapter 1).

4. Federal law now stipulates that areas that observe daylight saving time begin at 2:00 A.M. on the first Sunday in April and end at that time on the last Sunday in October.

5. See, for example, California Energy Commission, "Effects of Daylight Saving Time on California Electricity Use," Staff Report no. P400-01-013, May 2001.

6. Ignoring the large segment of nonideological, pragmatic, independent voters, some pundits view the razor-thin margin of the 2000 presidential election as reflecting a deep, close 50-50, red-blue, Republican-Democrat division that is now semipermanent. Such a split would increase the chances of presidential contests being so close that extremely early projections are impossible.

7. Westerners could adjust their polling hours to add time in the morning and close slightly earlier (perhaps half an hour) in the evening. If westerners are unwilling to make such a change themselves, they cannot fairly ask others to make greater changes that are more costly and disruptive and may have unintended negative side effects.

References

Abramson, Paul R., and John H. Aldrich. 1982. "The Decline in Electoral Participation in America." *American Political Science Review* 76 (September): 502–521.

Adams, William C. 1978. "Local Public Affairs Content of Television News." *Journalism Quarterly* 55 (Winter): 690–695.

———, ed. 1981. *Television Coverage of the Middle East.* Norwood, N.J.: Ablex.

———, ed. 1982. *Television Coverage of International Affairs.* Norwood, N.J.: Ablex.

———, ed. 1983. *Television Coverage of the 1980 Presidential Campaign.* Norwood, N.J.: Ablex.

———. 1984. "Media Power in Presidential Elections: An Exploratory Analysis of 1960–1980." In *Media Power in Politics,* ed. Doris Graber, pp. 175–185. Washington, D.C.: Congressional Quarterly Press.

———. 1985a. "The Beirut Hostages: ABC and CBS Seize an Opportunity." *Public Opinion* 8 (August–September): 45–48.

———. 1985b. "Convention Coverage." In *The Mass Media in Campaign '84,* ed. M. J. Robinson and Austin Ranney, pp. 10–15. Washington, D.C.: American Enterprise Institute.

———. 1987. "As New Hampshire Goes . . ." In *Media and Momentum,* ed. Gary Orren and Nelson Polsby, pp. 42–59. Chatham, N.J.: Chatham House.

———. 2003. "Whose Lives Count?" In *Television: Critical Concepts in Media and Cultural Studies,* vol. 2, ed. Toby Miller, pp. 153–162. London: Routledge.

Adams, William C., and Suzanne Albin. 1980. "Public Information and Social Change: Television Coverage of Women in the Workforce." *Policy Studies Journal* 8 (Spring): 717–733.

Adams, William C., and William Lucas. 1977. *An Assessment of Telephone Survey Methods.* Santa Monica, Calif.: Rand.

Adams, William C., and Krystyn Schmerbeck. 2005. "West Coast Radio and Early Election Returns: 1984 and 2004." Unpublished research paper, George Washington University.

Adams, William C., and Fay Schreibman, eds. 1978. *TV Network News: Issues in Content Research.* Washington, D.C.: George Washington University.

Adams, William C., and Dennis J. Smith. 1980. "Effects of Telephone Canvassing on Turnout and Preferences: A Field Experiment." *Public Opinion Quarterly* 44 (Autumn): 389–395.

Adams, William C., and Ted J. Smith III. 2003. "Benchmarking World-Class Annual Reports." In *Communication Best Practices,* ed. Donald P. Cushman and S. King, pp. 81–101. Albany: State University of New York Press.

Ansolabehere, Stephen, and Shanto Iyengar. 1995. *How Political Advertisements Shrink and Polarize the Electorate.* New York: Free Press.

Bardach, Eugene. 2000. *A Practical Guide for Policy Analysis.* New York: Chatham House.

Biemer, Paul, Ralph Folsom, Richard Kulka, Judith Lessler, Babu Shah, and Michael Weeks. 2003. "An Evaluation of Procedures and Operations Used by the Voter News Service for the 2000 Presidential Election." *Public Opinion Quarterly* 67 (Spring): 32–44.

Boyd, Richard W. 1989. "The Effects of Primaries and Statewide Races on Voter Turnout." *Journal of Politics* 51 (August): 730–739.

Brainard, Lori. 2003. *Television: The Limits of Deregulation.* Boulder: Lynne Rienner.

Campbell, Donald, and J. Stanley. 1963. *Experimental and Quasi-Experimental Designs for Research.* Chicago: Rand McNally.

Committee for the Study of the American Electorate. 1999. *Final Post Election Report.* Available at http://www.gspm.org/csae/cgans5.html.

Danielson, Wayne A. 1956. "Eisenhower's February Decision: A Study of News Impact." *Journalism Quarterly* 33 (Fall): 433–441.

Delli Carpini, Michael X. 1984. "Scooping the Voters? The Consequences of the Networks' Early Call of the 1980 Presidential Race." *Journal of Politics* 46 (February–March): 866–885.

Deutschmann, Paul, and Wayne Danielson. 1960. "Diffusion of Knowledge of the Major News Story." *Journalism Quarterly* 37 (Summer): 345–355.

Downs, Anthony. 1957. *An Economic Theory of Democracy.* New York: Harper Collins.

Dubois, Phillip L. 1983. "Election Night Projections and Voter Turnout in the West: A Note on the Hazards of Aggregate Data Analysis." *American Politics Quarterly* 11 (July): 349–364.

"Election Night Projections." 1984. *ISR Newsletter* (Spring–Summer): 4–5.

Epstein, Edward Jay. 1973. *News from Nowhere.* New York: Random House.

Epstein, Laurily, and Gerald Strom. 1981. "Election Night Projections and West Coast Turnout." *American Politics Quarterly* 9 (October): 479–491.

———. 1984. "Survey Research and Election Night Projections." *Public Opinion* 7 (February–March): 48–50.

Farnsworth, Stephen J., and S. Robert Lichter. 2003. *The Nightly News Nightmare: Network Television's Coverage of U.S. Presidential Elections, 1988–2000.* Lanham, Md.: Rowman and Littlefield.

Fern, Edward F., and Edward E. Fern. 2001. *Advanced Focus Group Research.* Thousand Oaks, Calif.: Sage.

Fine, Gary Alan. 1975. "Recall of Information about Diffusion of a Major News Event." *Journalism Quarterly* 52 (Winter): 751–755.

Folkert, Jean. 2000. "An Editorial Comment." *Journalism and Mass Communication Quarterly* 77 (Autumn): 452.

Frankovic, Kathleen. 2003. "News Organizations' Responses to the Mistakes of Election 2000." *Public Opinion Quarterly* (Winter): 19–31.

Fuchs, Douglas A. 1965. "Election Day Newscasts and Their Effects on Western Voter Turnout." *Journalism Quarterly* 42 (Winter): 22–28.

———. 1966. "Election Day Radio-Television and Western Voting." *Public Opinion Quarterly* 30 (Summer): 226–236.

Fuchs, Douglas A., and Jules Becker. 1968. "A Brief Report on the Time of Day When People Vote." *Public Opinion Quarterly* 32 (Fall): 437–440.

Gantz, Walter. 1983. "Diffusion of News About the Attempted Reagan Assassination." *Journal of Communication* 33 (Winter): 56–67.

Gantz, Walter, Kathy A. Krendl, and Susan R. Robertson. 1986. "Diffusion of a Proximate News Event." *Journalism Quarterly* 63 (Summer): 282–287.

Glynn, Carroll J., Andrew F. Hayes, and James Shanahan. 1997. "Perceived Support for One's Opinions and Willingness to Speak Out: A Meta-Analysis of Survey Studies on the 'Spiral of Silence.'" *Public Opinion Quarterly* 61 (Autumn): 452–463.

Graber, Doris. 1988. *Processing the News: How People Tame the Information Tide.* New York: Longman.

Hill, Richard J., and Charles M. Bonjean. 1965. "News Diffusion: A Test of the Regularity Hypothesis." *Journalism Quarterly* 41 (Summer): 336–342.

Hunter, John E., and Frank L. Schmidt. 1995. *Methods of Meta-Analysis.* Newbury Park, Calif.: Sage.

Jackman, Robert W. 1987. "Political Institutions and Voter Turnout in Industrial Democracies." *American Political Science Review* 81 (June): 405–423.

Jackson, John E. 1981. *Media Predictions and Voter Turnout in the United States, Election Day 1980.* Conducted by Market Opinion Research. ICPSR ed. Ann Arbor, Mich.: Interuniversity Consortium for Political and Social Research. Computer file.

———. 1983. "Election Night Reporting and Voter Turnout." *American Journal of Political Science* 27 (November): 615–635.

Jackson, Robert A. 1996. "A Reassessment of Voter Mobilization." *Political Research Quarterly* 49 (June): 331–349.

Jamieson, Kathleen Hall, and Paul Waldman. 2002. "The Morning After: The Effect of the Network Call for Bush." *Political Communication* 19 (January–March): 113–118.

Joslyn, Richard, Marc Ross, and Michael Weinstein. 1984. "Election Night News Coverage: Limits of Story-Telling." *PS* 17 (Summer): 564–571.

Kennamer, J. David. 1987. "How Media Use During Campaign Affects the Intent to Vote." *Journalism Quarterly* 64 (Summer): 291–300.

Key, V. O. 1963. *Public Opinion and American Democracy.* New York: Knopf.

Kohut, Andrew. 1986. "Rating the Polls: The Views of Media Elites and the General Public." *Public Opinion Quarterly* 50 (Spring): 1–10.

Konner, Joan. 2003. "The Case for Caution: The System Is Dangerously Flawed." *Public Opinion Quarterly* 67 (Spring): 5–18.

Konner, Joan, James Risser, and Ben Wattenberg. 2001. *Television's Performance on Election Night 2000: A Report for CNN.* Available at http://www.cnn.com/2001/allpolitics/stories/02/02/cnn.report/cnn.pdf.

Krippendorf, Klaus. 1981. *Content Analysis: An Introduction to Its Methodology.* Beverly Hills, Calif.: Sage.

Krueger, Richard A., and Mary Anne Casey. 2000. *Focus Groups: A Practical Guide for Applied Research.* Thousand Oaks, Calif.: Sage.

Lacy, Dean, and Barry Burden. 1999. "The Vote-Stealing and Turnout Effects of Ross Perot in the 1992 U.S. Presidential Election." *American Journal of Political Science* 43 (Spring): 233–255.

Lang, Kurt, and Gladys Engel Lang. 1968. *Voting and Nonvoting: Implications of Broadcasting Returns Before Polls Are Closed.* Waltham, Mass.: Blaisdell.

Lau, Richard, Lee Sigelman, Caroline Heldman, and Paul Babbitt. 1999. "The Effects of Negative Political Advertisements." *American Political Science Review* 93 (December): 851–875.

Levy, Mark R. 1983. "The Methodology and Performance of Election Day Polls." *Public Opinion Quarterly* 47 (Spring): 54–67.

Lott, John R. 2001. "Documenting Unusual Declines in Republican Voting Rates in Florida's Western Panhandle Counties in 2000." SSRN Electronic Paper Collection: http://ssrn.com/abstract=276278.

Lucas, William, and William C. Adams. 1978. "Talking, Television, and Voter Indecision." *Journal of Communication* 28 (Autumn): 120–131.

Lyons, William, and Robert Alexander. 2000. "A Tale of Two Electorates: Generational Replacement and the Decline of Voting in Presidential Elections." *Journal of Politics* 62 (November): 1014–1034.

Mason, Linda, Kathleen Frankovic, and Kathleen Hall Jamieson. 2001. *CBS News Coverage of Election Night 2000: Investigation, Analysis, Recommendations.* New York: CBS News.

McDonald, Michael P. 2003. "On the Overreport Bias of the National Election Study Turnout Rate." *Political Analysis* 11 (1): 180–186.

McDonald, Michael P., and Samuel Popkin. 2001. "The Myth of the Vanishing Voter." *American Political Science Review* 95 (December): 963–974.

Mendelsohn, Harold. 1966. "Election-Day Broadcasts and Terminal Voting Decisions." *Public Opinion Quarterly* 30 (Summer): 212–225.

Mendelsohn, Harold, and Irving Crespi. 1970. *Polls, Television, and the New Politics.* Scranton, Pa.: Chandler.

Merkle, Daniel M., and Murray Edelman. 2000. "A Review of the Voter News Service Exit Polls from a Total Survey Error Perspective." In *Election Polls, the News Media, and Democracy,* ed. Paul J. Lavrakas and Michael W. Traugott, pp. 68–92. New York: Chatham House.

Miller, Delbert C. 1945. "Research Note on Mass Communication." *American Sociological Review* 10 (October): 691–694.

Miller, Warren E. 1992. "The Puzzle Transformed: Explaining Declining Turnout." *Political Behavior* 14 (1): 1–43.

Mitofsky, Warren. 1991. "A Short History of Exit Polls." In *Polling and Presidential Election Coverage,* ed. Paul J. Lavrakas and Jack K. Holley, pp. 83–99. Newbury Park, Calif.: Sage.

———. 1995. "A Review of the 1992 VRS Exit Polls." In *Presidential Polls and the News Media,* ed. Paul J. Lavrakas, Michael W. Traugott, and Peter V. Miller, pp. 81–100. Boulder: Westview.

———. 1998. "Was 1996 a Worse Year for Polls than 1948?" *Public Opinion Quarterly* 62 (Summer): 230–249.

———. 2001. "Fool Me Twice: An Election Nightmare." *Public Perspective* (May–June): 35–38.

———. 2003. "Voter News Service After the Fall." *Public Opinion Quarterly* 67 (Spring): 45–58.

Morrison, David E. 2003. *The Search for a Method: Focus Groups and the Development of Mass Communication Research.* Luton, UK: University of Luton Press.

National Commission on Federal Election Reform. 2001. *Final Report of the Commission.* Charlottesville: Miller Center of Public Affairs, University of Virginia.

Neuendorf, Kimberly A. 2001. *The Content Analysis Guidebook.* Newbury Park, Calif.: Sage.

Oliver, Eric, and Raymond E. Wolfinger. 1999. "Jury Aversion and Voter Registration." *American Political Science Review* 93 (March): 147–152.

Patterson, Thomas E. 1980. *The Mass Media Election.* New York: Praeger.

———. 1993. *Out of Order.* New York: Alfred A. Knopf.

———. 2002. *The Vanishing Voter.* New York: Alfred A. Knopf.

———. 2003. *Diminishing Returns: A Comparison of the 1968 and 2000 Election Night Broadcasts.* Cambridge: Shorenstein Center, Harvard University.

Patterson, Thomas E., and Robert McClure. 1976. *The Unseeing Eye.* New York: Putnam.

Pepper, Robert. 1973–1974. "Election Night 1972: TV Network Coverage." *Journal of Broadcasting* 18 (Winter): 27–38.

Perrin, Daniel B. 2001. "Testimony on Federal Elections." U.S. Senate Committee on Government Affairs on Federal Elections. May 3.

Pierce, Caroline. 2001. "Election 2000: Examining the Consequences of an Overanxious Media." Unpublished paper. Rhodes College.

Quarles, Rebecca, Leo W. Jeffres, Carlos Sanchez-Ilundain, and Kent Neuwirth. 1983. "News Diffusion of Assassination Attempts on President Reagan and Pope John Paul II." *Journal of Broadcasting* 27 (Fall): 387–395.

Riker, William, and Peter C. Ordeshook. 1968. "A Theory of the Calculus of Voting." *American Political Science Review* 62 (March): 25–42.

Robinson, Michael J. 1976. "Public Affairs Television and the Growth of Political Malaise." *American Political Science Review* 70: 409–432.

Robinson, Michael J., and Margaret A. Sheehan. 1983. *Over the Wire and On TV: CBS and UPI in Campaign '80*. New York: Sage.

Rosenstone, Steven. 1982. "Economic Adversity and Voter Turnout." *American Journal of Political Science* 26 (February): 25–46.

Rosenstone, Steven, and Raymond Wolfinger. 1978. "The Effect of Registration Laws on Voter Turnout." *American Political Science Review* 72 (March): 22–45.

Rosenthal, Robert. 1991. *Meta-Analytic Procedures for Social Research*. Newbury Park, Calif.: Sage.

Sammon, Bill. 2001. *At Any Cost: How Al Gore Tried to Steal the Election*. Washington, D.C.: Regnery.

Schur, L., and D. Kruse. 2000. "What Determines Voter Turnout? Lessons from Citizens with Disabilities." *Social Science Quarterly* 81 (2): 571–587.

Schwartz, David A. 1973. "How Fast Does News Travel?" *Public Opinion Quarterly* 37 (Winter): 625–627.

Sheatsley, Paul B., and Jacob Feldman. 1964. "The Assassination of President Kennedy." *Public Opinion Quarterly* 28 (Summer): 189–215.

Shepard, Alicia C. 2001. "How They Blew It." *American Journalism Review* (January–February): 20.

Sobel, Russell S., and Robert A. Lawson. 2000. "Did the Media's Early Call of Florida for Gore Change the Election?" West Virginia University Working Paper no. 01-07.

Southwell, Priscilla L., and Marcy Everest. 1998. "The Electoral Consequences of Alienation." *Social Science Journal* 35 (1): 43–52.

Squire, Peverill, Raymond E. Wolfinger, and David P. Glass. 1987. "Residential Mobility and Voter Turnout." *American Political Science Review* 81 (March): 45–66.

Straits, Bruce C. 1990. "The Social Context of Voter Turnout." *Public Opinion Quarterly* 54 (Spring): 64–73.

———. 1991. "Bringing Strong Ties Back in Interpersonal Gateways to Political Information and Influence." *Public Opinion Quarterly* 55 (Autumn): 432–448.

Sudman, Seymour. 1983. "The Network Polls: A Critical Review." *Public Opinion Quarterly* 4 (Winter): 490–496.

———. 1986. "Do Exit Polls Influence Voting Behavior?" *Public Opinion Quarterly* 50 (Autumn): 331–339.

Tannenbaum, Percy, and Leslie Kostrich. 1983. *Turned-On TV, Turned-Off Voters: Policy Options for Election Projections.* Beverly Hills, Calif.: Sage.

Teixeira, Ruy A. 1992. *The Disappearing American Voter.* Washington, D.C.: Brookings Institution.

Thompson, Dennis. 2002. *Just Elections.* Chicago: University of Chicago Press.

Tichenor, Philip, George Donohue, and Clarice Olien. 1970. "Mass Media Flow and Differential Growth in Knowledge." *Public Opinion Quarterly* 34 (Summer): 159–170.

Timpone, Richard. 1998. "Structure, Behavior, and Voter Turnout in the United States." *American Political Science Review* 92 (March): 145–158.

Tolbert, Caroline J., John A. Grummel, Daniel A. Smith. 2001. "The Effects of Ballot Initiatives on Voter Turnout in the American States." *American Politics Research* 29 (November): 625–648.

Tuchman, Sam, and Thomas Coffin. 1971. "The Influence of Election Night Broadcasts on Television in Close Elections." *Public Opinion Quarterly* 35 (Fall): 315–326.

U.S. Bureau of the Census. 1990. *Studies in the Measurement of Voter Turnout.* Current Population Reports, Series P-23, no. 168. Washington, D.C.: U.S. Government Printing Office.

Weaver, Paul. 1975. "Newspaper News and Television News." In *Television as a Social Force,* ed. Douglas Cater and Richard Adler, pp. 81–94. New York: Praeger.

Weber, Robert P. 1990. *Basic Content Analysis.* Newbury Park, Calif.: Sage.

West, Mark D. 2001. *Theory, Method, and Practice in Computer Content Analysis.* Norwood, N.J.: Ablex.

Wielhouwer, Peter W. 1994. "Party Contact and Political Participation, 1952–90." *American Journal of Political Science* 38 (February): 211–229.

———. 2000. "Releasing the Fetters: Parties and the Mobilization of the African-American Electorate." *Journal of Politics* 62 (February): 206–222.

Wilson, David B., and Mark W. Lipsey. 2000. *Practical Meta-Analysis.* Thousand Oaks, Calif.: Sage.

Wilson, Paul. 1983. "Election Night 1980 and the Controversy over Early Projections." In *Television Coverage of the 1980 Presidential Campaign,* ed. William C. Adams, pp. 141–160. Norwood, N.J.: Ablex.

Winders, B. 1999. "The Roller Coaster of Class Conflict: Class Segments, Mass Mobilization, and Voter Turnout in the U.S., 1840–1996." *Social Forces* 77 (March): 833–862.

Wolfinger, Raymond, and Peter Linquiti. 1981. "Tuning In and Turning Out." *Public Opinion* (February–March): 56–60.

Wolfinger, Raymond, and Steven Rosenstone. 1980. *Who Votes?* New Haven: Yale University Press.

Wright, Gerald C., Jr. 1975. "Black Voting Turnout and Education in the 1968 Presidential Election." *Journal of Politics* 37 (May): 563–568.

Yalch, Richard F. 1976. "Pre-Election Interview Effects on Voter Turnout." *Public Opinion Quarterly* 40 (Autumn): 331–336.

Zipp, John F. 1985. "Perceived Representativeness and Voting." *American Political Science Review* 79 (March): 50–61.

Index

1960 election, 2, 6, 13, 39–40
1964 election, 2, 6, 9, 13, 40,
1968 election, 2, 6, 13, 40
1972 election, 2, 6, 13, 27, 41
1976 election, 13, 97, 100
1980 election, 2, 6, 9, 11, 13, 27, 41,
    96–98, 100
1984 election, 2, 4, 6, 7, 9, 13, 43,
    44, 47, 59–63, 72, 85–91, 93,
    96–98, 100
1988 election, 2, 4, 6, 7, 13, 48–49,
    81, 98
1992 election, 2, 4, 6, 13, 49–50
1996 election, 2, 4, 6, 13, 50, 96–98,
    100
2000 election, 2, 4, 6, 9, 13, 50, 97,
    100, 113, 126, 128, 133, 135
2004 election, 2, 6, 8–9, 13, 51–54,
    57, 91, 97–100, 116, 120, 127,
    133–134

ABC, 6, 37, 40–46, 48–56, 81, 89,
    97, 106, 114, 121, 122, 124–126
Alabama, 122, 126
Alameda County, California, 82
Alaska, 3–4, 10, 21, 49, 60
Arizona, 121
Arkansas, 121, 126

Associated Press, 52, 57, 122
AuCoin, Les, 60, 71, 74

Barnes, Fred, 115
Beckel, Bob, 125
Bell, Steve, 56
Brinkley, David, 43, 55
Brokaw, Tom, 43, 45, 46, 49, 53,
    121
Brown, Pat, 83
Bush, George H. W., 2, 48–50, 81
Bush, George W., 2, 51–53, 113–126

California, 3, 4, 20–22, 26–28, 32,
    37, 40, 49, 60, 83, 103–104, 111,
    130, 133; Energy Commission,
    135; voter registration changes,
    26–29, 32, 95
Canada, 132
Carter, Jimmy, 2, 31–32, 35, 37,
    41–42, 50, 55, 72, 106
CBS, 1, 5, 8, 21, 32, 34, 37, 40–54,
    57, 62, 72, 81, 89, 97, 104–106,
    117–118, 121–122, 125
Census Bureau, 29, 32, 37, 46,
    76–77, 88, 93
Characterizations, 40, 45–46, 56
Cheney, Dick, 125

Clinton, Bill, 3, 49–50, 56, 72
CNN, 20, 51, 53, 54, 112, 115, 117, 120, 125–126
Colorado, 121, 126
Comparisons: of congressional districts, 34–35; of counties within the same state, 75–77, 85–91; of hourly trends, 78–80, 95–101, 115–117; of states and regions 26, 28–29, 32, 75, 85
Congress, U.S., 9–11, 22, 31, 34, 41–42, 45, 60–61, 71, 73, 86–87, 115, 122, 133–134
Content analysis, 39, 55–56; findings, 39–57, 118, 120–122
Corman, James, 22, 41

Daylight savings time, 21, 133–134
Delli Carpini, Michael, 25–26, 28, 34–35
Diffusion of news. *See* News diffusion
Dinnertime dropoff, 82–83, 95–96
Dole, Bob, 2, 50, 72
DrudgeReport.com, 51
Dubois, Philip, 25, 35, 55
Dukakis, Michael, 2, 48, 81

Effect size, 24–25
Elections. *See under specific year*
Electoral votes, 3–5, 7–9, 30–40, 45, 47, 49, 54, 133, 135
El Paso, 21, 85, 92, 125
Epstein, Laurily, and Gerald Strom, 25, 28, 30–31, 36, 37
Equity. *See* Fairness toward westerners
Exit polls, 2, 42–43, 51–54, 122, 132, 134
Experiments: randomized field, 83, 97; natural, 75, 83

Fairness toward westerners, 11, 20, 108–109, 111, 129–130, 132–134

Florida, 3, 6, 20, 21, 37, 50–52, 111, 113–120, 123–126
Focus groups, 103–105; findings, 105–111
Folkert, Jean, 55
Ford, Gerald, 2, 41
Fox News, 51–54, 115, 117, 122, 125, 126
Framing: the projection debate, 9–12, 129–130; election night coverage, 54
Freedom of speech, of the press, 10, 110, 132
Fuchs, Douglas, 22, 25, 30, 34–35, 82

Georgia, 37, 121–122, 126
Goldschmidt, Neil, 20
Goldwater, Barry, 2, 21, 40
Gore, Al, 51–52, 111, 113–126
"Go vote" appeals, 44–45, 47–49, 54, 56–57
Grant County, Oregon, 76–84
Greenfield, Jeff, 53, 115, 120

Hannity, Sean, 51
Hansen, George, 87
Hatfield, Mark, 74
Hawaii, 1–4, 10, 21, 26, 41, 49, 60, 132
Hendricksen, Margie, 74
Hughes, Charles Everett, 127
Hume, Brit, 114
Huntley, Chet, 55

Idaho, 3–4, 20–21, 85–93, 128
Illinois, 3, 40
Indiana, 2–3
Intercoder reliability, 56
Internet blogs, 51–53
Iowa, 2, 5

Jackson, John, 25, 30–31, 36–37, 55
Jennings, Peter, 45, 48, 56, 110, 114

John McLaughlin and Associates, 117, 124
Johnson, Lyndon, 2, 40

Kansas, 3, 6, 20–21, 85–93, 120, 132
Kennedy, John, 2, 40
Kentucky, 2–3
Kerry, John, 2, 51–53, 57
Key, V. O., 63
KGW, 47
Knowledge gap hypothesis, 64

Lang, Kurt, and Gladys Lang, 22, 25, 30, 35, 41
Lieberman, Joseph, 125
Limbaugh, Rush, 51
Los Angeles (*also* Los Angeles County), 95, 99–100, 103, 104, 115–116, 123–124
Louisiana, 121, 126

Maine, 1, 121, 126
Malheur County, Oregon, 75–84
Markam, Robert, 78
McDonald, Michael, 12
Mendelsohn, Harold, 22, 25, 30, 33, 35
Meta-analysis, 24–26; findings, 25–37
Michigan, 3, 6, 43, 114, 121, 122, 126, 133
Minnesota, 121, 126
Missouri, 40, 121
Mitofsky, Warren, 49, 52, 57, 122, 133
Models of voter turnout. *See* Voter turnout, models of
Mondale, Walter, 2, 43, 44, 74, 89
Moshofsky, Bill, 60, 74
Moyers, Bill, 45
MSNBC, 51
Munro, Ralph, 20

National Commission on Federal Election Reform, 34

National Election Study (NES), 60, 72
NBC, 20, 37, 41–46, 51–54, 81, 89, 97, 106, 117, 121–122
Nebraska, 21
Network Election Service, 40
Nevada, 35, 52, 53
New Hampshire, 21
New Mexico, 126
News diffusion, 62–66; from friends, 65–66; of major events, 66; from radio, 65; speed of, 62–63; from television, 64
New York, 2, 5, 19, 85, 107, 108
Nixon, Richard, 2, 40–41
North Carolina, 35, 121–123, 126
North Dakota, 21, 85, 90–93, 128
Novak, Bob, 114

Ohio, 3, 41, 50, 52–53, 121–122
Orange County, California, 104, 106
Oregon, 3, 4, 20–22, 37, 46, 47, 49, 59–85, 103–104, 111, 127–128; reasons for intensive study, 60–61, 75
O'Reilly, Bill, 56
Osgood, Charles, 47

Parker, Alton, 41
Patterson, Thomas, 15, 54, 57, 124
PBS, 51
Pennsylvania, 3, 52, 114, 121, 126
Perot, Ross, 2, 50, 56
Poll closing times, 2–5, 21; in dual time zone states, 3, 21, 75–76, 85–86, 117–120. *See also* Uniform poll-closing proposals
Portland, 46–47, 56, 59–74, 104
Projections: after all or most polls closed in a state, 3, 6–8, 10, 120, 133–134; delayed for certain states in 2000, 120–123; delayed for certain states in 2004, 52–53; objections to, 9–12, 129–134;

predictors of exposure to, 64;
timing of, 1–2, 39–50, 127,
133–134. *See also* Exit polls

Quayle, Dan, 48

Radio, 46–48, 51, 55, 57, 64–65,
124
Rather, Dan, 1, 43–45, 48, 53, 56,
118, 124
Reagan, Ronald, 2, 21, 41, 43, 46,
56, 60–71, 74, 83, 89
Rhode Island, 2, 5, 56
Rockefeller, Nelson, 21
Roosevelt, Teddy, 41
Russert, Tim, 115, 122

Sammon, Bill, 115
San Diego, 20, 104
Schrum, Bob, 124
Seattle, 20, 104
Shock theory (only unexpected
projections matter), 59–60
Slate.com, 51
South Carolina, 35
South Dakota, 21
Sudman, Seymour, 25–26, 31, 34,
36, 55, 59
Survey research, 25, 29–32, 34–37,
55, 110–112, 117, 124;
challenges, 30–33, 69–70;
Portland area findings, 35,
59–74; Portland area methods,
61–62, 72–73
Swift, Al, 10, 22

Tauzin, Billy, 122
Tennenbaum, Percy, and Leslie
Kostrich, 25, 30–31, 33–36, 101,
130
Tennessee, 21, 121
Texas, 3, 6, 35, 50, 85, 125, 133
Today Show, 53

Tuchman, Sam, and Thomas Coffin,
55

Ullman, Al, 22, 60–61
Uniform poll-closing proposals, 10,
20, 110, 131–132

Vermont, 121
VNS. *See* Voter News Service
Voigt, Carol, 78
Voter News Service (VNS), 57, 122,
126
Voter registration lists, 26–30,
34–35, 70–71, 73, 78–79, 88–89,
91, 95, 118–119, 125
Voter turnout: in California, 82–83,
95–100; in eastern Oregon,
78–82; in Kansas and Idaho,
89–90; models of, 17–19;
motivation and influences,
14–17, 67–70; in North Dakota,
90–91; in Portland area, 69–71,
73; trends, 12–14. *See also*
Survey research, challenges;
Voter registration lists; Voting-
age population; Voting-eligible
population
Vote switching, 11, 29
Voting. *See* Voter turnout
Voting-age population, 13, 26, 28,
30, 35, 46, 73, 90–91, 99
Voting-eligible population, 13, 28,
35, 99

Wallace, George, 2, 46
Washington (state), 3–4, 20, 49, 60,
103–104, 111, 121, 126
Westin, David, 6
West Virginia, 126
Wilson, Paul, 42–43
Wisconsin, 44, 92
Wolfinger, Raymond, and Peter
Linquiti, 25, 30–32

About the Book

In eight of the past dozen presidential elections, TV networks proclaimed the winner while citizens on the West Coast, Hawaii, and Alaska were still casting ballots. Is this a problem? Do early projections decrease voter turnout? Carefully examining data from every presidential election held from 1960 through 2004, William Adams definitively answers both questions.

Adams employs a range of methods (including content analysis, focus groups, survey research, meta-analysis, and time-series analysis) to corroborate his surprising finding that projections do not in fact discourage voter turnout—but do raise serious issues of equity and discrimination. His persuasive analysis suggests clear policy options designed to keep voters from feeling discounted and devalued on election day.

William C. Adams is professor of public policy and public administration at George Washington University.